Contents

Nature Is Determined	7
Chapter 1: The Animal that Thought It Ruled the World	17
Chapter 2: Why Our World is Green	33
Chapter 3: The Wolves that Grew Trees and Healed Rivers	49
Chapter 4: Into the Wild Wood	61
Chapter 5: Why You Should Give a Dam About Beavers	78
Chapter 6: Whales Are Climate Warriors	91
Chapter 7: Can We Raise Woolly Mammoths from the Dead?	104
Chapter 8: How to Feed the World	116
Chapter 9: How You Can Help the Wild	132
Can We End the Anthropocene?	142
Our Rewilding Planet – in the Year 2050	147
Glossary	151
Index	156
Acknowledgements	159
About the Author and Illustrator	160

EXPLODAPEDIA
REWILD
Can Nature Heal Our World?

Ben Martynoga

Illustrated by
Moose Allain

d|b
David Fickling Books

Explodapedia: *Rewild*
is a
DAVID FICKLING BOOK

First published in Great Britain in 2024 by
David Fickling Books,
31 Beaumont Street,
Oxford, OX1 2NP
EU Rep: Authorised Rep Compliance Ltd., Ground Floor,
71 Lower Baggot Street, Dublin, D02 P593,
Ireland.
www.arccompliance.com

Text © Ben Martynoga, 2024
Illustrations © Moose Allain, 2024

978-1-78845-277-9

5 7 9 10 8 6 4

The right of Ben Martynoga and Moose Allain to be identified as the author
and illustrator of this work has been asserted in accordance with the
Copyright, Designs and Patents Act 1988.

All rights reserved. No part of this publication may be reproduced, stored in a
retrieval system, or transmitted in any form or by any means, electronic,
mechanical, photocopying, recording or otherwise, without the prior
permission of the publishers.

Papers used by David Fickling Books are from well-managed forests and other
responsible sources.

DAVID FICKLING BOOKS Reg. No. 8340307

A CIP catalogue record for this book is available from the British Library.

Printed and bound in Great Britain by Clays, Ltd, Elcograf S.p.A.

Italic type is used in *Explodapedia* to highlight words that are defined in the glossary when they first appear, to show quoted material and the names of published works. Bold type is used for emphasis.

Nature Is Determined

Did you see that weed growing from the crack in the pavement?
Or the freckled butterfly next to the trainline?
Did you spot the falcon nesting high up on that skyscraper?
Or brush against the moss under the bridge?
And did you notice the trees springing up on the
abandoned building site?

Nature doesn't wait for an invitation. It has a habit of just arriving, whether we like it or not.

Some farmers' fields provide an all-you-can-eat buffet for mice, songbirds – and the odd swarm of locusts. And all sorts of smaller 'pests' – ants, moths, flies, cockroaches and moulds – pop up unprompted inside our homes. Meanwhile, larger creatures make their presence felt on city streets across the globe . . .

In recent years, leopards have even been seen loping through parts of Mumbai, India, and in the UK, after dark, foxes throw parties in London gardens.

Nature has zero respect for private property.

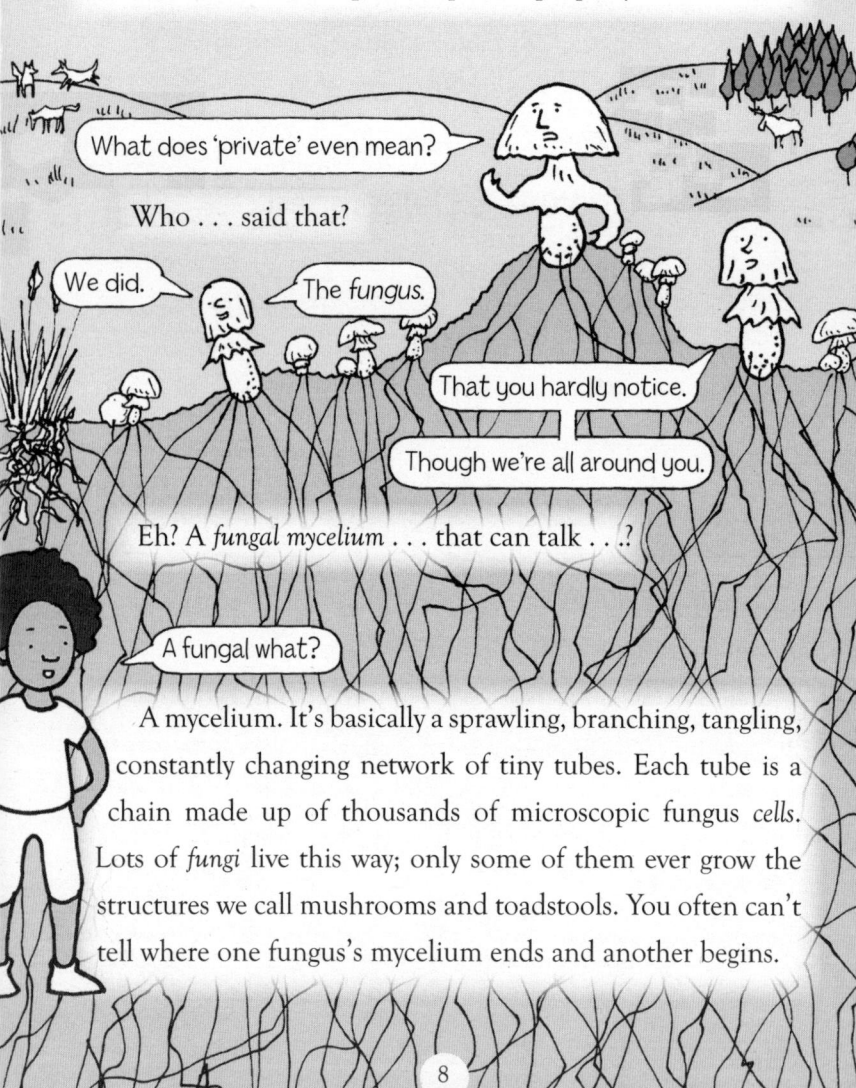

What does 'private' even mean?

Who . . . said that?

We did.

The *fungus*.

That you hardly notice.

Though we're all around you.

Eh? A *fungal mycelium* . . . that can talk . . .?

A fungal what?

A mycelium. It's basically a sprawling, branching, tangling, constantly changing network of tiny tubes. Each tube is a chain made up of thousands of microscopic fungus *cells*. Lots of *fungi* live this way; only some of them ever grow the structures we call mushrooms and toadstools. You often can't tell where one fungus's mycelium ends and another begins.

The wild creatures that surround us come in an eye-wateringly massive variety of living forms, from the tiniest *bacteria* to wasps, tree frogs, jellyfish, cacti, fruit bats, toadstools and corals to the tallest redwood trees, and everything else in between. Biologists call these and all other living things *biodiversity*, which literally means 'variety of life'. Our planet's biodiversity is unimaginably enormous: there may be up to a trillion different *species* out there, no one knows for sure. But each one has found its own unique way to hang on to life and, when it gets a chance, to **flourish**.

Don't be fooled though. Despite the amazing determination of wild things, and the stupendous range of species, all is not well with our planet's biodiversity.

Nature in Peril

Species go *extinct* all the time. They always have; they always will. But the awful truth is that today, extinctions are happening at a terrifying rate. In some parts of the world so many species of plant, animal, fungus and *microbe* are **disappearing** that landscapes and seas that once thrummed with wildlife are falling eerily still and silent.

The last time Earth's biodiversity shrank so quickly was 66 million years ago, when a gigantic meteorite slammed into our planet, snuffing out the dinosaurs and 75% of all other species.* We're not quite at that point yet - thank goodness - but we need to act now, before too many other life forms vanish for ever.

*Apart from the dinosaurs we now call 'birds' (see *Explodapedia: Evolution*).

Sadly, our fungal friend is basically right. For centuries, most people have been so focused on our own needs, that we've scarcely noticed the harm all our human activities have been doing to the rest of the living world. The reality is, we're in the middle of a *biodiversity crisis*.

WE NEED NATURE

They sure do. As you might know, biologists call the communities of plants, animals, fungi and other forms of life that exist in a particular place an *ecosystem*. Ecosystems are made up of both **living** parts (e.g. plants, animals and bacteria) and **non-living** parts (e.g. water, rock, weather conditions). All the different parts of an ecosystem are connected. So if one part changes – e.g. a storm blows in or an animal goes extinct – that change can affect **everything else** in the ecosystem.

The living species in a healthy ecosystem have often been evolving alongside each other for millions of years. Despite all the eating – and being eaten – that goes on, they fit together like the pieces of a beautiful puzzle.

Ecosystems can be very small, like a tide pool at the seaside:

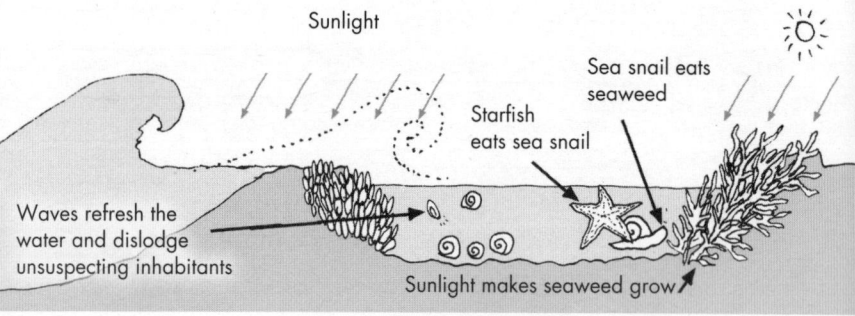

Or very large, like an entire ocean:*

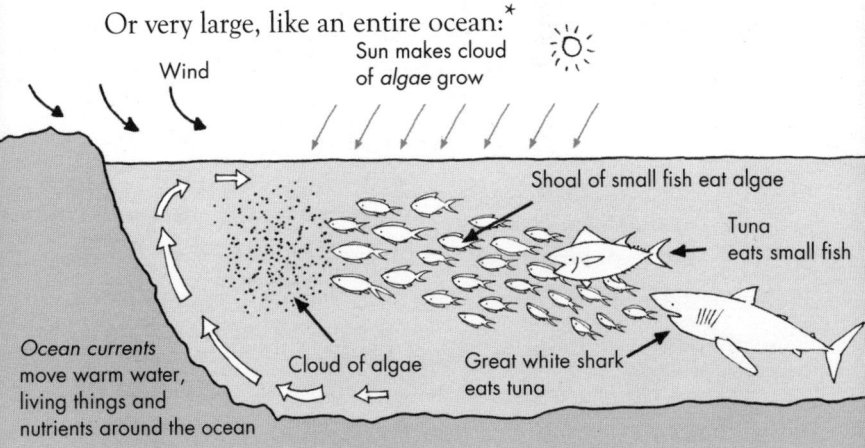

And together, ecosystems have awesomely powerful effects on entire environments. We'll see, as we read on, how they basically act as a life-support system – for us and for all other living things.

We can **rewild** as much of the world as possible. That's what this book is all about. It means getting better at living

* Large ecosystems are sometimes called 'biomes', they often contain many smaller ecosystems.

alongside nature and, where appropriate, backing right off and letting *natural processes* take control. Because, when we let it, nature comes roaring back.

Trust us! Sometimes, we wild things know best.

A Half-Wild World

But what will happen to our towns, cities and farms if we let everything go back to nature?

Well, we don't have to give it **all** back. *Rewilding* is about mending our broken relationship with nature – remembering that we are **part** of nature, that we **need** nature.

How much to rewild is definitely up for debate. But in 2016, one of the world's leading biologists, Edward O. Wilson, hatched a daring plan. He called it the 'Half-Earth Project':

*I propose that only by committing **half** of the planet's surface to nature can we hope to save the immensity of life forms that compose it.*

In other words, he reckoned we should confine all our building, farming and other human-focused activities to, at most, 50% of Earth's surface. And that would mean putting the other 50% back into the capable hands (not to mention paws, roots, wings, fins and tendrils) of nature.

If we did that, Wilson calculated, we'd protect **85%** of Earth's species from extinction.

We're a **long** way from hitting that goal though. In 2023, less than **17%** of the planet's total surface (land, freshwater, ice and ocean) was officially protected for nature.*

The trouble is, as well as the biodiversity crisis, we're wrestling with the equally terrifying *climate crisis*. As our planet gets hotter, weather systems are becoming increasingly violent and unpredictable. Wildfires, *droughts*, storms and rising water temperatures are hammering ecosystems, making the biodiversity crisis worse.

But here's the thing: since natural ecosystems – from jungles to *peatlands* to seaweed forests to frozen Arctic *tundra* – help to keep the climate stable, if the biodiversity crisis gets worse,

*And simply saying a site is 'protected' isn't enough – to actually help wildlife, rules must be enforced and, often, work done to improve habitats.

the climate crisis will too. If we don't do something – and quickly – both crises will spiral out of control.

> Then you'll really be in a mess.

We certainly will. But the good news about rewilding is that it's part of the solution to the climate crisis too.

> So, let's get on with it!

Actually, rewilding projects are already underway all over the world. We're about to get to know some of the scientists, conservationists, local communities and, most importantly, other species that are doing their utmost to usher **life** back into our wounded world. Plus, we'll look at some of the ways these efforts to rewild will help **you** and how **you** can help **them**.

But first of all, we've got to face up to some dark realities . . .

CHAPTER 1
The Animal that Thought It Ruled the World
HOW WE GOT INTO THIS MESS

Rewilding is all about healing our damaged world by boosting the biodiversity and *abundance* of its living species. But, before we can find out how the solutions work, we need to understand the problems. This chapter's not going to be an easy read, but stick with it, because knowing all the challenges the world is facing actually gives us an amazing opportunity. If we can welcome enough of the wild back into our landscapes, our oceans and our day-to-day lives, we'll be the first generation of humans ever to have **attempted** to leave the planet in a better state than it was when we arrived.

I want to be part of that! So - deep breath - tell it like it is.

The Relentless Rise of the Human

In 2021, builders on a new housing estate near Plymouth, south-west England, unearthed a hidden cave. Inside were the remains of woolly mammoths, reindeer, wolves, hyenas and woolly rhinoceroses – animals that are either long extinct, or haven't lived in Britain for centuries. These bones give us a way of seeing Britain as it must have been around 40,000 years ago, during the last Ice Age.

A human jawbone found in a nearby cave shows that during the same period, modern humans (i.e. *Homo sapiens*) were reaching Britain for the very first time. By that point our species had already existed for about 250,000 years, but for most of that time our ancestors had all lived in Africa. So, 40,000 years ago, intrepid bands of *hunter-gatherers* were on the move, gradually occupying the rest of the world.

Compared with the way you live today, life was unrecognizably different for your ancestors 1,500 generations ago. On every continent, temperatures were typically five or six degrees Celsius **colder** than today's, and ice, up to a mile thick, covered huge parts of the globe. As sliding glaciers scoured the rocks, they stirred up clouds of rock dust that dimmed the sun and fell in drifts across the wintry landscapes.

In short, life was tough. And humans were just another kind of fairly insignificant animal.

We barely noticed you back then!

Exactly. It was a far wilder age, and your human ancestors would never have doubted that they were **part of nature**. At any moment, a blizzard, a *cave lion* or even a small infected cut could have brought life to an abrupt end. As a result, the human population of the entire planet was about the same as that of a large town today.

But, against the odds, humans clung on and, eventually, the population started to grow. By pooling ideas, controlling fire and inventing more effective tools and weapons, they began to clear patches of forest and have a bigger impact on the wildlife around them.

Then, around 11,000 years ago, the Ice Age finally ended. As the climate became less harsh, some groups of people started to farm, burning and hacking their way through more forest to create their fields. Eventually, around 9,000 years ago, the global population swelled to around 10 million (the same as Portugal today), and the first cities appeared.

Over the centuries, humans built towering pyramids and mighty castles; they formed religions; fought wars; used sailing ships, carts, camels and mules to shift themselves and their goods from place to place, while their horses and oxen ploughed up ever more land. As our ancestors' knowledge grew, a dangerous new idea started to spread: that human beings were **separate** from the rest of nature.

> What nonsense! You were always part of nature, just like us.

Of course. It only took a few failed harvests or a deadly disease to remind people that they were still at nature's mercy – during the 1300s a disease pandemic known as the Black Death killed around 25% of all people alive at the time.

Despite regular setbacks, the human population managed to keep growing, slowly but surely. Then, around 250 years ago, everything suddenly started to speed up as we entered the Industrial Age. Newly invented coal-powered steam engines could

work non-stop, 24/7, with far more power than any human or other animal. Huge factories sprang up, iron railways snaked across continents and mighty steamships plied the oceans. Gas lights were soon illuminating streets and homes, further separating the human world of towns and cities from nature.

Then, roughly 150 years ago, the first oil wells were dug and the first electric power stations were built. And the pace of change got **even faster**. Gigantic herds of cars, ships and planes began to roar around the globe. Tractors hauled, bulldozers cleared, chainsaws hacked. More roads were built. More trees were felled. More fish netted. And, *hectare* by hectare, more and more wild land was **tamed**.

> **That's** when we really started to notice you...

The Industrial Age brought all sorts of benefits for many humans. With more food and medicines available, people started living longer, healthier lives. As they spent less time shivering, hiding from predators and growing their own food, more and more people started to believe that they had a right to take whatever they wanted from the natural world. And they didn't think twice about dumping their waste all over it.

At this point most people didn't just start to see themselves as separate from nature, they began to think they could **control** nature, that they were in **charge** of it.

And in some ways, we humans really have taken charge . . .

WELCOME TO THE *ANTHROPOCENE*

In 2020 scientists worked out that all the human-made things in the world – i.e. all houses, supermarkets, electricity pylons, motorways, umbrellas, chopsticks, used nappies, books, iPhones, fake lawns, inflatable unicorns and everything else – are now heavier than the combined weight of **all the world's living things** – including every single blade of grass, tree, whale, fish, worm, parrot, cow, octopus, ant and bacteria. In other words, we've strewn our stuff all over the globe.

Our impact on the planet has become so massive that scientists call the current period of Earth's history the *Anthropocene epoch* – which is Greek for 'the new age of the humans'.

What?! The age of the humans? But you've only just got here.

True. Life has existed on Earth for about four billion years. Our species, *Homo sapiens*, has been here for 'just' 300,000 years. To see how recent that is, imagine life's entire history as a 4,000 metre running race, with new species joining in once they evolve on Earth:

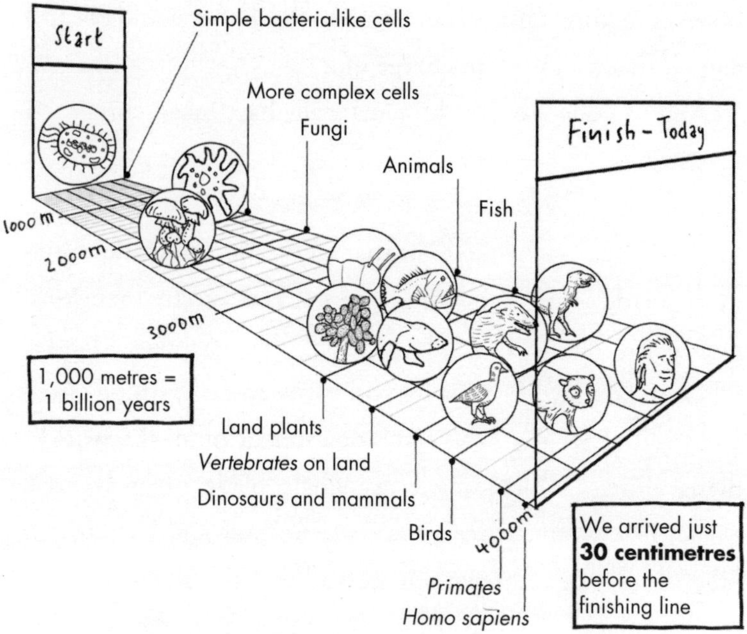

Start
- Simple bacteria-like cells
- More complex cells
- Fungi
- Animals
- Fish

1000 m / 2000 m / 3000 m

1,000 metres = 1 billion years

- Land plants
- *Vertebrates* on land
- Dinosaurs and mammals
- Birds
- Primates
- Homo sapiens

Finish – Today

We arrived just **30 centimetres** before the finishing line

The Industrial Age played out during the final **quarter millimetre** of the race

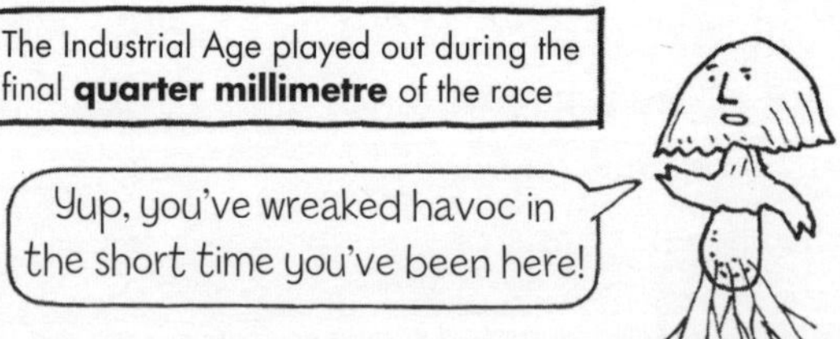

Yup, you've wreaked havoc in the short time you've been here!

That's why having a geological epoch named after us isn't anything to be proud of. Over the last two centuries our population has **exploded** to over eight billion (a two million per cent rise since the Ice Age). And it's still rising. During this time, our frantic activity has sparked both the biodiversity crisis **and** the climate crisis.

Before we can work out how exactly rewilding can fix things, we should take a closer look at how they got broken. Be prepared – this won't be pretty. Here's a crash course on the main causes of the **two biggest challenges** facing the world during the Anthropocene.

Global Challenge Number One: The Biodiversity Crisis

A recent *United Nations* report warns that up to a million plant and animal species are at risk of extinction in the coming decades – because of human activities. Here are the five main causes of this carnage.

1. Habitat Destruction

Humans clear forests to make way for more crops and livestock, build dams that can wreak havoc on rivers and other freshwater ecosystems, and farm in ways that cause billions of tonnes of soil to be washed or blown away each year. All living things struggle to survive when the habitats they live in shrink or disappear.

2. Pollution

Pollution from human activities now affects **every** ecosystem on Earth. For example, the *fertilizers* farmers spread on their fields can create *dead zones* in rivers, lakes and seas (see p. 84), and *pesticides* are one of the main reasons insect numbers are plummeting around the world (see p. 124). Plastic waste that ends up in the oceans can have devastating effects on all kinds of marine life.

3. *Invasive Species* and Diseases

As people and goods criss-cross the planet like never before, other living things often travel with us – accidentally and intentionally. These can become invasive species that grow out of control, causing problems for local wildlife, for example:

- Water hyacinths from South America now grow in at least 50 other countries. They can form a thick green layer that stops sunlight and oxygen reaching other water creatures.

- A fungus that spread around the world on the skins of exported tropical frogs has become the **most deadly disease** ever discovered – at least for *amphibians*. So far, it has driven over 90 species to extinction.

• Even your pet cat (originally from the Middle East) is an invasive predator. Scientists estimate that pet cats threaten over 400 species of bird, mammal and reptile globally.

4. (Too much) Fishing and Hunting

For most of our history, hunting, trapping and fishing have been vital for our survival. But today there are **billions** of us. And catching wild animals is not a sustainable way to feed everyone.

• Marine scientists say that at least one-third of the world's fish populations are crashing because of over-fishing.

• A huge 2021 study looked at dozens of bird, mammal and reptile species that are caught for their meat, kept as pets or used in traditional medicines. The conclusion was clear: populations of wild animals involved in the global wildlife trade are shrinking fast.

The **fifth** main cause of biodiversity loss is also our second global challenge: the climate crisis. Here it is in a nutshell.

Global Challenge Number Two: The Climate Crisis
1. The Greenhouse Effect

The *greenhouse gases* – e.g. *carbon dioxide* (CO_2), *methane*, *nitrous oxide* and *water vapour* – exist at low levels in Earth's *atmosphere*.

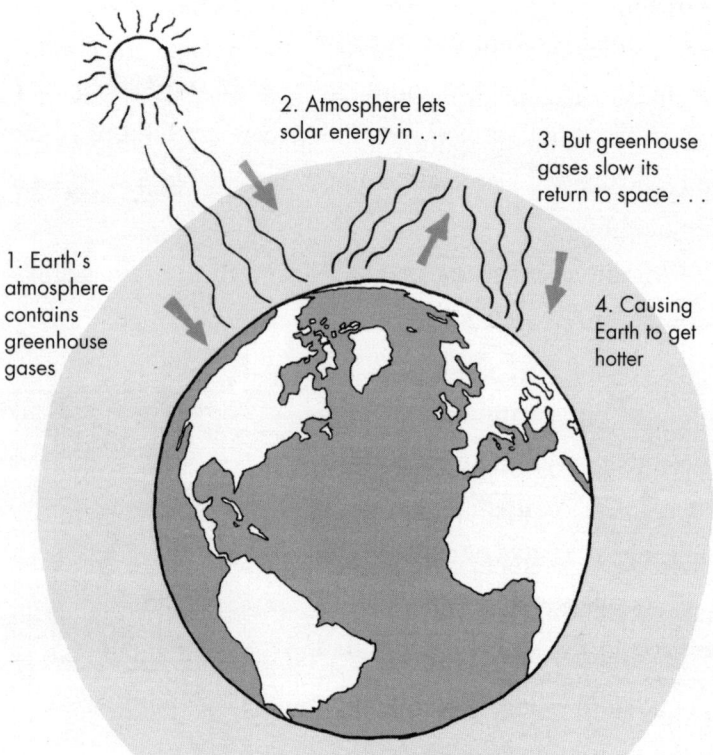

Like the glass in a greenhouse roof, greenhouse gases let *solar energy* from the sun **in**, but stop some of it returning immediately to space, after it bounces **off** the planet's surface.

Without greenhouse gases, Earth's surface would be around −18 degrees Celsius and life as we know it would be impossible.

During the Industrial Age, human activities started producing these gases in truly colossal amounts and today . . .

2. Greenhouse Gas Levels Are STILL Rising

Around **three-quarters** (73%) of all human-made greenhouse gas emissions come from burning *fossil fuels* (coal, oil and natural gas), which produce most of the energy that keeps our world moving, as well as a stupendous amount of carbon dioxide gas.

We've pumped enough extra greenhouse gases into the air to raise average temperatures by more than one degree Celsius since the 1800s. That might not sound like much of a jump, but it's already altering weather patterns and causing more extreme storms, droughts, heatwaves and wildfires. It's making life harder for hundreds of millions of people across the globe. And it's taking its toll on our planet's ecosystems. For example:

• Bush fires in Australia during 2019–20 scorched an area nearly the size of the whole of New Zealand, killing or displacing three billion mammals, birds, reptiles and amphibians. Fires like these are becoming more common and destructive.

• Sea levels are rising and oceans are becoming warmer and slightly more acidic, damaging coral reefs and many other marine life forms.

And if we don't act soon . . .

3. Things Could *Much* Worse

Many climate scientists are really anxious about '*positive feedback loops*': changes to the climate that trigger further changes that make the climate crisis worse and worse, like this one involving sea ice in the Arctic Ocean:

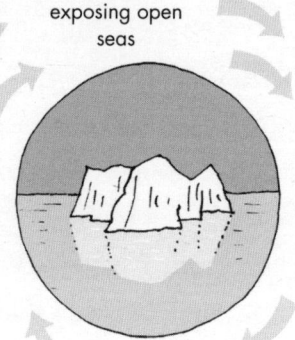

Ice melts, exposing open seas

Surface of sea water is now dark, so it absorbs more solar energy

Even more ice melts, exposing even more dark water

Temperature and sea levels rise

Feedback loops often involve wild ecosystems. If lots of them kicked in at the same time, they could push the climate past a series of irreversible *tipping points*.

These **could** be real headlines by the early 2100s:

TEMPERATURES UP BY SCORCHING 4.5 DEGREES CELSIUS

ARTIC ICE CAPS VANISH FOR EVER

WILDFIRE CATASTROPHE: BILLIONS OF ANIMALS PERISH

FAILED HARVESTS TRIGGER REFUGEE CRISIS

AMAZON RAINFOREST DESTROYED

WORLD'S CORAL REEFS NEARLY ALL GONE

NEW YORK SWAMPED BY RISING SEA LEVELS

> That's completely terrifying, these are humongous challenges!

It's the reason we need to act **now**. We still have time to stop it becoming reality. And right now, the biodiversity and climate crises are making each other **worse**. We need to take urgent action on both – which is where rewilding really can help.

By now, most of us understand that the main thing we need to do to slow down the climate crisis is to wean ourselves off fossil fuels.

Far fewer people know that rewilding could be **just as important**. Biodiverse ecosystems have the power to both slow the climate crisis **and** help living things cope when the climate changes in the future.

When it comes to protecting and, wherever possible, **increasing** the variety and abundance of our planet's priceless biodiversity, rewilding – like crazy – is 100% our best hope.

> Get on with it, then!

> Let's REWILD!

Right. But if this is going to work, we humans have got to remember that we're as much a part of the natural world today as our ancestors were back in the last Ice Age. And no amount of fancy technology will change the simple fact that, if the ecosystems that sustain us die, we die.

Now we know how things got messed up, it's time to get to grips with how nature goes about its business, filling our world with colour and life.

So let's venture boldly . . . into the wild.

CHAPTER 2
Why Our World Is Green
THE RULES OF NATURE

If we truly want rewilding to succeed, we've got to encourage huge parts of the world to fill up with throngs of diverse life forms that can get on with their planet-sustaining work, without any interference from us humans. But to turn that dream into reality, we need to learn absolutely everything we can about how nature works.

Let's start by travelling back to 1921, to visit an island in the Svalbard archipelago, hundreds of miles north of the Arctic Circle.

It's summer, but a savage wind is raking the half-frozen landscape. And, whoops, someone has just fallen through a patch of sea ice!

Our shivering hero is twenty-one-year-old biology student, Charles Elton, and he's just been saved by his backpack. Phew!

Elton's never been abroad before, let alone anywhere as wild as this and, amazingly, the fall doesn't put him off. After warming up at his expedition base camp, he gets straight back to work, identifying **all** the island's animals and plants. Why?

I want to understand how living things cling on in an extreme environment.

What's more, some animals, like the flocks of guillemots, fulmars, puffins and other seabirds that nest on the cliffs, seem to be positively thriving.

The investigations this young scientist-in-training does here will shape a new, world-changing branch of science: *ecology*.

To make sense of this place, Elton realizes he's got to **follow the food**! And there isn't much of that to go round. For example, plants can only grow across the 10% of the island where the ice melts during the summer months.

Elton starts to map out the way food flows from one *organism* to the next:

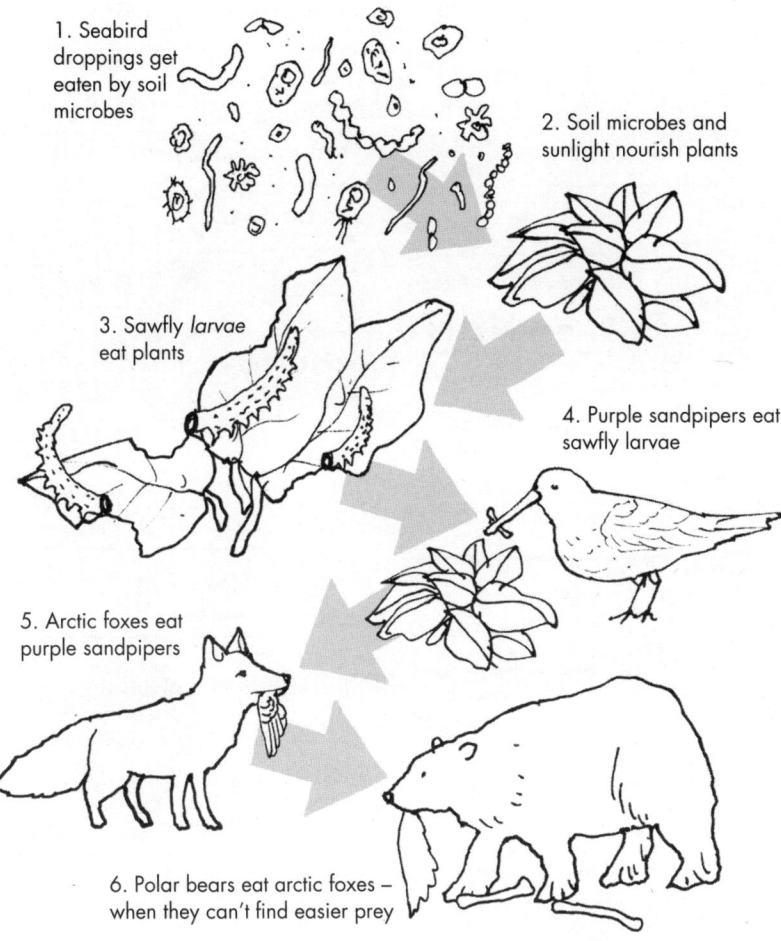

1. Seabird droppings get eaten by soil microbes
2. Soil microbes and sunlight nourish plants
3. Sawfly *larvae* eat plants
4. Purple sandpipers eat sawfly larvae
5. Arctic foxes eat purple sandpipers
6. Polar bears eat arctic foxes – when they can't find easier prey

This, as you probably know, is a *food chain*. Elton invented – and named – this powerful new way of understanding the natural world.

And he went on to map out every food chain on Svalbard that he could, before heading back to university, in Oxford, UK, and linking them together into a *food web*. Like this:

Arrows indicate who feeds who

Crikey. There's a lot going on!

Yep. But it's much simpler than the food web in the Amazon rainforest, say, which has **millions** of different species jostling for resources!

That's why Svalbard was an inspired staring point: Elton was able to understand how **every species** fitted together.

Elton helped the scientific world see that similar basic patterns apply to all food webs, in all ecosystems. Nowadays, for example, ecologists simplify food webs by dividing the living world up into three main kinds of organism, based on how they get their food:

1. **Producers** are an essential part of all ecosystems because they make their **own** food. All organisms need energy, and it's the producers that suck that energy into their food webs, keeping all the other species around them going. On land, the most vital producers are usually plants. In the water, the main producers are algae (including seaweeds) and microbes called *phytoplankton*. They each grow by capturing the sun's energy through *photosynthesis*.

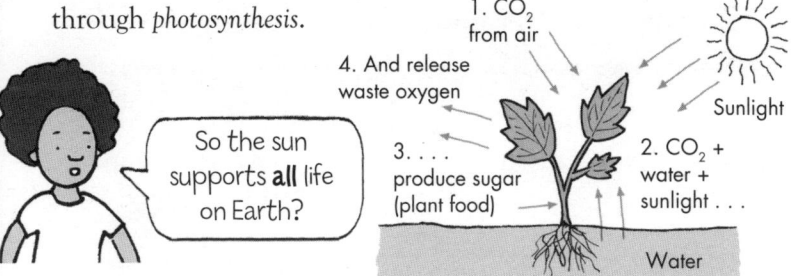

So the sun supports **all** life on Earth?

1. CO_2 from air
2. CO_2 + water + sunlight . . .
3. . . . produce sugar (plant food)
4. And release waste oxygen

Sunlight

Water

Well, nearly all. Some producers are microbes that live in places the sun doesn't reach, like volcanic areas deep beneath the seas. Instead of sunlight, they suck chemical energy into their food webs.

2. **Consumers** can't make their own food, so they eat other organisms instead. Consumers can be:

- *herbivores* (plant eaters)

- *carnivores* (meat eaters)

- *omnivores* (eat various different kinds of organism)

- *parasites* (including organisms that cause diseases. They feed on the bodies of other living things without bothering to kill them or wait for them to die).

3. **Decomposers** are the living world's ultimate recyclers. They include a huge range of fungi, bacteria, worms, insects and other small animals. They get their energy and nutrients by feeding on the dead bodies and waste products left behind by other living things.

Dead right, Fungus. Decomposers actually keep all plants and most other producers going. If they didn't exist, dead bodies and *faeces* would just pile up **everywhere**. And the chemical nutrients inside them would be locked away for ever. Soils wouldn't form, and before long all food webs would run out of nutrients and **everything** would die.

See?

LIVING PYRAMIDS

In 1926 Elton made another huge leap. He showed that the organisms in a food chain usually make up what he called a 'pyramid of numbers' (today it's called a *trophic pyramid* – 'trophic' means 'relating to food'). The organisms on each level of a trophic pyramid get their energy by feeding on organisms in the levels below. The pyramid shape is because energy gets 'wasted' at each trophic level. For example, when herbivores move around, chew and digest, they use up energy – so there's less energy for the consumers higher up the chain. That's why there are usually fewer individuals at the higher levels of a trophic pyramid.

Here's a trophic pyramid based on one of Elton's Arctic food chains.

Trophic Level

Level 5. **Apex predators** – e.g. polar bears – perch at the top. Often eco-systems can only support a few apex predators. Humans are the only species that hunt them

Parasites and disease-causing organisms (called *pathogens*) feed on **every trophic level**.*

Level 4. **Larger carnivores or omnivores** – e.g. Arctic foxes

Level 3. **Carnivores or omnivores** – e.g. purple sandpipers, which eat insects and plants

Level 2. **Herbivores** – e.g. sawfly larvae, which eat plants

Level 1. **Producers** – plants, *lichens* and algae that get energy through photosynthesis (see p. 37)

Level 0. **Decomposers** – e.g. bacteria, worms and fungi in the soil. They support the entire pyramid by scavenging nutrients and energy from the higher levels and feeding them to plants

> Couldn't creatures high up the food chain just gobble up **all** the plants and animals below them?

*Even the biggest predators suffer from infections.

Well, if **every** creature ate everything in the trophic level below, some species would probably go extinct. But it's a good point. The green stuff at the bottom of a food web can't run away, so why isn't it grazed to death?

A group of ecologists asked a very similar question back in 1960 . . .

Why Is Our World Green?

It's been debated fiercely ever since. Scientists have come up with lots of possible explanations, but they generally fall into two main categories:

1. **Bottom-Up Regulation**: Sometimes plants don't provide enough nutrients to allow herbivore numbers to get big enough to wipe them out entirely. But also, while plants can't leg it when they see a goat or leaf-cutter ant coming, they have evolved all sorts of ways to outwit hungry herbivores. For example, they can:

- Defend themselves with thick bark, spines and thorns.
- Fill their leaves with poisons.
- Make seeds or roots that can lie dormant, then sprout once the herbivores have moved on.

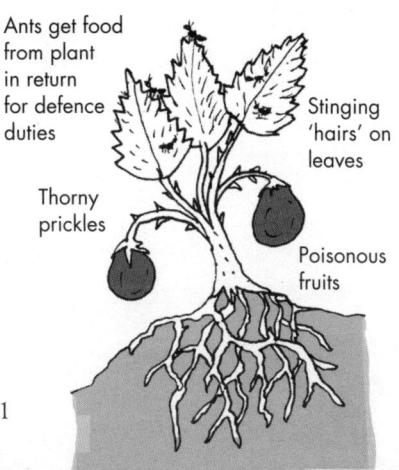

Scaryplantus explodapedius

Ants get food from plant in return for defence duties

Stinging 'hairs' on leaves

Thorny prickles

Poisonous fruits

2. **Top-Down Regulation**: When herbivores eat a lot of plants, their population will usually grow. But that's also good news for predators, who can move in on the extra herbivores, like kids attracted to an ice-cream van, and start gobbling them up. That way, the predators push the herbivore population back down, giving the plants a break. Diseases can do something similar. By reducing herbivore numbers plants can bounce back.

Won't SOMEBODY save us?!

So, in most ecosystems, plants' green shoots and leaves seem to survive because bottom-up **and** top-down regulation keep herbivore numbers at a safe level. Actually, the other trophic levels work in a similar way: populations are usually controlled by what's happening below them **and** above them.

But even the disappearance of just one species can have dramatic effects that ripple right through food webs.

THE *KEYSTONE SPECIES* THAT SUPPORT ENTIRE ECOSYSTEMS

In 1971 a young biologist called Jim Estes was studying the wildlife of the Aleutian Islands, off the Alaskan coast, in the North Pacific Ocean. The first island he visited, Amchitka, was overflowing with wild creatures:

Next, he sailed to Shemya Island, 200 miles to the west. Shemya had a similar geology and climate, but – compared to Amchitka – it was a wildlife desert:

Otter-skin coats had been massively popular in the 19th century, and in the North Pacific otters were hunted almost to extinction for their fur. Otter hunting was banned in 1911, thank goodness, and by the time Estes visited the Aleutian Islands, sea otters were making a comeback, slowly breeding and spreading along Alaska's coast and islands.

But they hadn't reached Shemya Island yet. And Estes realized that the otters were the single species that made all the difference to these island ecosystems.

Wherever there are otters, the kelp forests are thriving.

Cool. But the otters couldn't literally make seaweed grow, could they?

No. But they ate a **lot** of urchins. And urchins are herbivores, so **they** ate a **lot** of kelp. After the otters had been killed off, the urchins reproduced in such huge numbers that they gobbled up all the kelp. Kelp was the main producer (see p. 37) on Shemya, so the island's ecosystem basically collapsed without it. The surrounding seabed was left chock full of urchins, some starfish and not much else.

No living species can keep guzzling the planet's resources for ever!

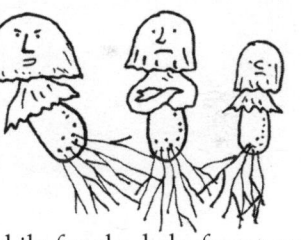

Are you listening, humans?

It's a fair point! And, luckily for the kelp forest ecosystem, the otters returned. Then they took control of the urchins, from the 'top down' (see p. 42), so the kelp grew back – and their world turned green (well, greenish-brown!) again. And once the kelp was thriving, all manner of fish, small sea creatures, seals and birds could flourish again too. That one change high up in the food web (the return of the otters) had effects that echoed through **every** other trophic level.

Ecologists call this a *trophic cascade*. And they call species that have these dramatic, and often surprising, effects on whole ecosystems keystone species. Just like the keystones that hold up stone bridges, entire food webs can **fall apart** when one keystone species is removed. Jim Estes proved that sea otters were one of the main keystone species supporting the ecosystems of the North Pacific.

Why We Need to Know the Rules of Nature

So, the survival of otters determined the survival of kelp that determined the survival of fish that determined the survival of seabirds and bald eagles.

When it comes to ecosystems, complexity is their superpower. It's also the reason we should seriously worry about species going extinct in our biodiversity crisis.

> Do we have to keep going back to the bad news?

Sorry, but that's kind of why we're here. And it's important to remember that a complicated ecosystem is – usually – a healthier and more stable ecosystem. If a food web has lots of different species at a particular trophic level, it can keep working well, even if one species, or more, moves away or goes extinct – there's always another species on hand to do a similar 'job'. This is particularly crucial when ecosystems get damaged, e.g. by the climate crisis or pollution. If biodiversity is high, ecosystems can take a knock – like a storm, fire, drought, flood or disease outbreak – and keep on functioning just fine. But when biodiversity starts to fall, an ecosystem can suddenly collapse.

Think of a complex machine like a plane. The *rivets* that hold it together are like the species in an ecosystem. A plane is usually built with more rivets than it actually needs, which means the plane can often keep flying even if several of those rivets pop out. But if at some point it loses a particularly crucial rivet, the whole plane will fall apart and plummet from the skies. The same goes for ecosystems that either lose too many species, or just their keystone species.

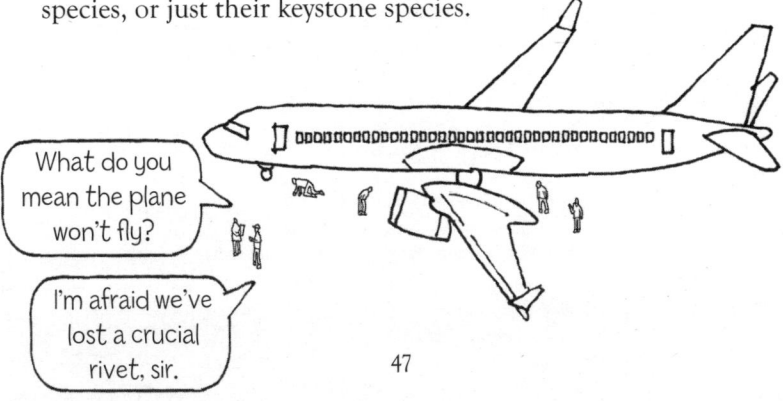

However, unlike planes, some damaged ecosystems can basically regrow their own 'rivets'. For that to happen, sometimes we just have to step back and let species do their thing.

It won't always work. If hunting hadn't been banned and the otters hadn't returned to the North Pacific, the kelp forests would never have regrown - there were just too many sea urchins around.

But, thanks to Charles Elton, and all the other brilliant ecologists who have followed in his footsteps, we now know how to figure out the rules of an ecosystem. And that means we can pinpoint its most important 'rivets' - including its keystone species - and pop them back into place.

Rewilding is essential, but that doesn't mean it's easy. Putting the wrong species in the wrong place at the wrong time can do more harm than good. But, if we learn the 'rules of nature', we're much less likely to make that mistake. And, when the right creature arrives in the right place at the right time, nature can heal itself, sometimes to an almost miraculous degree - as we're about to find out.

CHAPTER 3
The Wolves that Grew Trees and Healed Rivers
WHY ECOSYSTEMS NEED FEROCIOUS PREDATORS

Winter 1995, Yellowstone National Park, Montana, USA
See those golden eyes peering out from the crate?

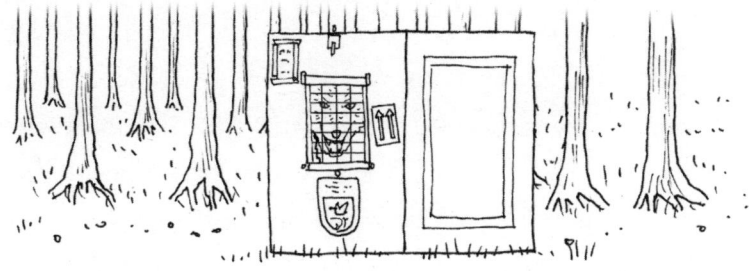

They belong to one of the most magnificent predators ever to have evolved: a grey wolf. The park rangers are about to set her free, along with 13 of her kind. They think the wolves' killer instincts and razor-sharp teeth will usher **more life** into this landscape.

Wolves prowled these hills, forests and valleys for millions of years – until their reign suddenly ended in the 1920s.

Oh? What happened?

Yellowstone was the world's very first national park. It was created in 1872. But the people in charge wanted rid of the wolves.

Eh? I thought national parks were all about **protecting** wildlife?

Funnily enough, it doesn't always work like that. Back at the turn of the 20th century, lots of people thought wolves were dangerous, bloodthirsty creatures. The Yellowstone National Park Service was worried that wolves would terrorize day trippers and hikers. Local farmers also complained about having to protect their sheep and cattle. And then there were the hunters who came to Yellowstone to shoot elk – they didn't want wolves catching too many and ruining their sport.

In reality, wolves are shy creatures – attacks on humans were, and still are, extremely rare. Yes, hungry wolves will sometimes eat lambs or calves, but farmers and shepherds had been protecting their flocks in wolf country for thousands of years. And as for the hunters, well, there were plenty of elk around for both them and the wolves to prey on.

But the decision was made, and Yellowstone's last native wolf was shot in 1926.

So until the first animals were re-released there, in 1995, there hadn't been any wolves in Yellowstone for nearly 70 years. The national park's wildlife hadn't exactly collapsed at this point. But more and more ecologists had been arguing for years that its ecosystems had a massive wolf-shaped hole and were suffering as a result. Here's how part of the park looked just **before** the wolves came back:

Big herds of elk roam freely, without fear of predators

Just one small colony of beavers

Elks' favourite food is young trees and shrubs, so aspen, willow, cottonwood trees and berry bushes cannot grow in some areas

With less plant cover, bare river banks suffer erosion

Coyotes (smaller relatives of the wolf) roaming in large packs have pushed down the numbers of pronghorn antelope, hare, rabbit and small rodents

It's a bit like the trophic cascade that transformed the otters' ecosystem (see p. 46). The wolves are also a keystone species. When they returned to the top of their trophic pyramid there were knock-on effects that rippled throughout their food web. Reducing elk numbers helped trees grow, beavers multiply and all kinds of other wild things to flourish.

The wolves created opportunities for creatures to thrive at every single trophic level, from the grizzly bears towards the top of the pyramid down . . .

... to us lot in the soil ...

... keeping the whole place going.

For example – and this is slightly gruesome – when wolves kill an elk, its carcass becomes an entire new ecosystem.

1. Bears, ravens, magpies and eagles compete for leftover body parts

2. Decomposers (see p. 38), including maggots, beetles and a massive array of fungi and bacteria, break down the remains of the corpse

3. Beetles and maggots provide food for birds and small mammals

4. Nutrients dripping from the carcass feed fungi and soil microbes

5. Richer soil means bigger plants will grow on this patch of ground, attracting more herbivores and therefore more predators, and so on up the food chain

What a feast!

Believe it or not, some biologists think that even Yellowstone's elk are better off, thanks to the wolf. In the past, elk populations sometimes used to boom. Then, during the winter, they often ran out of food and thousands of them would die, slowly and agonizingly, from hunger and cold. That doesn't really happen these days. The wolves pick off the weakest elk and stop the population swinging up and down. The remaining elk are tougher and wilier.

In fact, ecologists think the wolves have made the whole park more resilient. With denser tree cover (see Chapter 4), healthier rivers and wetter habitats (see Chapter 5), it should be better able to withstand the extreme weather and forest fires that the climate crisis is predicted to hurl at it in years to come.

Nope. Not so far. Besides, if the wolf population ever did

get too big, or individual wolves started causing trouble, park rangers could move in to control the problem predators.

> There you go again, thinking you can control everything.

Well, with our guns and traps, we humans have basically become the planet's ultimate apex predator. But unlike all other top predators, we no longer need to hunt wild animals to survive. What's more, we understand that most ecosystems can only recover when their (non-human) apex predators return. So, even if those predators (very) occasionally threaten us, it's often worth the risk. Because complete ecosystems that can look after themselves without our involvement will also look after us, and the rest of the planet.

Can Predators Work their Magic Elsewhere?

In a 2018 study, scientists estimated that across the globe, 64% of large carnivore species, from wild hunting dogs to snow leopards, are threatened with extinction, and 80% have shrinking populations.

As with wolves, in the past, fear has often driven people to attempt to kill predators off. But the organisms that sit at the top of their trophic pyramids can also suffer most when their ecosystems are damaged or their habitats destroyed. There are three main reasons for this.

- Their populations are usually quite small (see pp. 39-41).
- They tend to breed quite slowly compared to animals at lower trophic levels.
- They often have larger bodies, so they need a lot of food and large areas to hunt in.

The news isn't all bad for big carnivores though. Inspired by the incredible effects triggered by the return of wolves to Yellowstone and sea otters to the North Pacific (see pp. 43-6), lots of projects are looking to rewild habitats by bringing back long-lost apex predators. For example, tigers are making, ahem, a **roaring** comeback in parts of China,

endangered crocodiles are being let loose in swamps in the Philippines, and California condors are once again soaring over the west coast of the USA.

The consequences of releasing ruthless carnivores into the wild can be hard to predict, and the risks to other wildlife – and to people – can be significant. But these quick case studies highlight some of the problems that occur when predators disappear, and how their return can be a large part of the solution.

1. Bringing Back the Vultures

The problem: During the 1990s, the populations of vultures in India, Nepal and Pakistan crashed by up to 99%, with no explanation. And without vultures to tidy up, cattle and wild

animal carcasses were left to rot.* This enabled wild dog and rat populations to soar, causing horrible diseases (e.g. rabies and anthrax) to spread in humans and wildlife. Leopards also crept into villages and towns to hunt the dogs. Sometimes they attacked people.

The solution: Scientists finally worked out that a medicine farmers fed their cows, called diclofenac, was poisoning the vultures when they ate the dead cattle. In 2006, diclofenac was finally banned and replaced with a safer drug. Since then there is evidence that some vulture populations are slowly recovering.

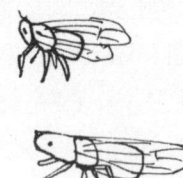

2. The Spiders that Help Rice Grow

The problem: In 1976, 400,000 hectares of rice paddies in Indonesia were attacked by small, plant-chomping insects called

---

*Though vultures are mainly scavengers, not predators, ecologists place them at the top of their food chains as 'apex carnivores'.

planthoppers. Farmers sprayed increasing amounts of pesticide chemicals on their rice crops to keep the insects at bay, but, to their horror, the planthoppers laid even more eggs and caused even worse damage! What the heck was happening?

The solution: The pesticides were more effective at killing the planthoppers' main enemies – including wolf spiders – than the planthoppers themselves.* With their predators out of the picture, the planthoppers could truly turn

into a plague. Using **less** pesticide and farming in ways that encouraged spiders and other natural predators to return and thrive helped prevent further attacks.

As usual, nature knows best.

3. If Wolves Aren't Welcome, What About Lynx?

The problem: Some conservationists have suggested re-introducing wolves to the Scottish Highlands to control deer numbers, thus encouraging new forests to grow and biodiversity to soar. But, like at Yellowstone 150 years ago, many farmers and landowners worry that wolves will kill too many sheep and threaten hill walkers.

---

*The planthoppers had evolved resistance to the insecticide. See *Explodapedia: Evolution* to learn more about how evolution works.

The solution: Lynx could be reintroduced instead. They're a bigger, stronger, wilder relative of our pet cats, that lived in Britain until around 700 CE. Lynx are even shyer than wolves, less likely to kill lambs and almost never known to attack people.

We Need the Top Dogs

Helping predators clamber back up to the tops of trophic pyramids can make a massive difference. But it isn't a miracle cure for every challenge facing the natural world. If we're serious about solving the biodiversity and climate crises, we've got to think about the health and well-being of organisms at every level, from the top to the bottom of the trophic pyramid.

We need to pay particularly close attention to a group of organisms whose branches, roots and leaves do so much to support life on Earth as we know it . . .

CHAPTER 4
Into the Wild Wood
THE TREES THAT SUPPORT LIFE ON LAND

Imagine someone invented a dirt-cheap, solar-powered machine that could suck huge amounts of CO_2 out of the air and store it in solid form? Make a lot of them and the climate crisis could be solved, right?

Well, about three trillion of those 'machines' already exist, although no one invented them. They're called trees.

> Trees are not machines! Trees are sacred. They breathe life into our world.

This is Txai Suruí. She belongs to the Suruí people. They've been living in and caring for a huge and gloriously wild part of the Amazon rainforest in the north of Brazil for at least 6,000 years.

And she's absolutely right. Trees **are** more amazing than any machine a human could invent.

They do so much to keep all of us – and most life on land – going.

In the face of the climate crisis, one of the most important things trees do is to snatch CO_2 out of the air and store it away, safely. Here's how:

1. Cells in leaves photosynthesize (see p. 37), converting CO_2, sunlight and water into sugar (which contains carbon and oygen)

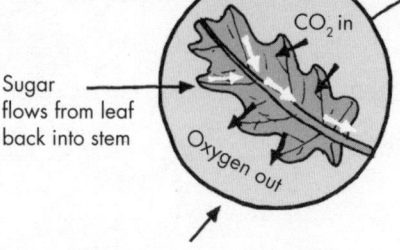

Sugar flows from leaf back into stem

CO_2 in

Oxygen out

2. Some sugar gives tree's cells the energy to live and grow

3. Some sugar is stored temporarily as starches in the branches and roots

Most of the oxygen we breathe is a waste product of photosynthesis

4. Carbon is stored more permanently by converting sugar into wood *molecules*

Burning fossil fuels is the **exact opposite** of photosynthesis. Coal, which launched the Industrial Age, is the fossilized remains of ancient forest trees. When we burn it, we're releasing CO_2 and solar energy that the trees locked away long ago, over the course of many millions of years

5. Huge amounts of carbon are also stored in soil. Fungi and microbes convert dead branches and leaves into the carbon-rich parts of soil

Each year the world's forests absorb almost a third of the CO_2 released by burning fossil fuels

Actually, that's literally true, and not just because they cast all that delicious shade. A big tree can be as cooling as **two** air conditioning units because of *evapotranspiration*, which works like this:

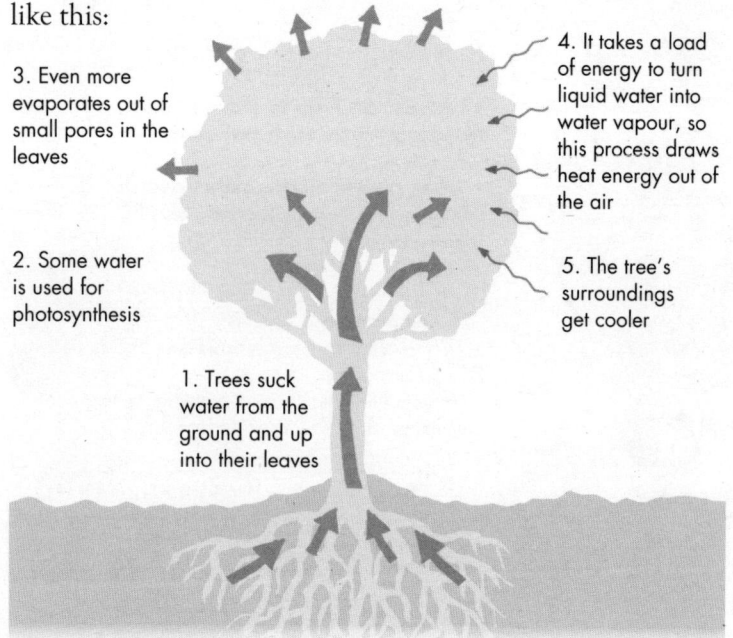

3. Even more evaporates out of small pores in the leaves

4. It takes a load of energy to turn liquid water into water vapour, so this process draws heat energy out of the air

2. Some water is used for photosynthesis

5. The tree's surroundings get cooler

1. Trees suck water from the ground and up into their leaves

And when lots of trees get together to form forests, some of the things they do are even more extraordinary.

The Flying Rivers of the Amazon

The Amazon is named after the huge river that weaves through the world's largest rainforest. But scientists have discovered even bigger rivers flowing through the **air** above the forest. These 'flying rivers' are created by the trees themselves . . .

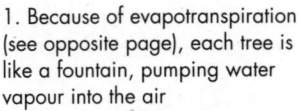

1. Because of evapotranspiration (see opposite page), each tree is like a fountain, pumping water vapour into the air

2. Wisps of vapour gather together, forming bigger streams of moist air that get blown across the forest and beyond

3. Trees keep the forest itself watered, by releasing special chemicals that trigger raindrops to form . . .

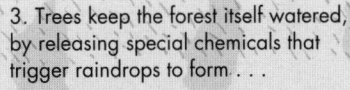

Wow – they literally put the 'rain' into 'rainforest'.

. . .and they only take a fraction of the water back

4. Flying rivers can flow for thousands of kilometres before falling to the ground as rain

The Amazon provides a lot of the rain that helps crops grow throughout South and Central America, and as far north as the Great Plains of the USA!

Tropical forests in Africa and in Southeast Asia create their own flying rivers that deliver vital rain to many of the world's biggest food-growing areas in North Africa, India, China and beyond.

See! Everyone depends on the forests that *Indigenous people* like me live in and look after.

Too true. Without the rain clouds those forests create, millions of people would starve.

> Flying rivers keep us wild things moist and happy too!

They absolutely do. We simply must make sure the world's tropical forests stay wild and healthy. Right now, we're failing on that score.

Rainforests in Peril

You've probably heard of *deforestation*. During 2021 alone, 11.1 million hectares of tropical forest were felled or deliberately burned – the equivalent of **52 football pitches every minute**. This is habitat destruction (see p. 25) on a terrifying scale.

> But why would anyone want to destroy a forest?

It's usually to clear land for raising cattle and planting crops, like oil palms and soy beans, without much thought about the consequences. Most of these foods get exported – they can turn up on supermarket shelves in every country. So we can't simply blame the farmers who are tearing down the forests – most of them are just trying to make a living, while big international food companies make huge profits. In short, we all need to be more aware of what we eat.

The other massive threat rainforests face is the climate crisis. Trees can't get up and move when they get too hot. Instead, they try to save water by shutting the pores in their leaves. That means they photosynthesize less (so absorb less CO_2) and stop feeding the flying rivers above them. That, in turn, can lead to a deadly, forest-killing, climate-heating 'positive feedback loop' (see pp. 30-1):

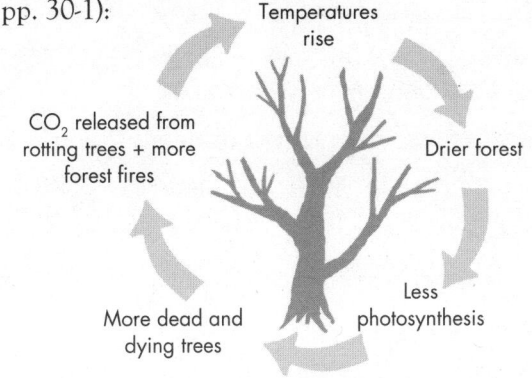

It seems this is already happening. In 2021–22, scientists discovered that large parts of the Amazon now release more CO_2 than they absorb! The entire rainforest – which has been growing non-stop for **55 million years** – could be rushing towards an unstoppable 'tipping point' (see p. 31). If things don't change fast, the Amazon could vanish in a few decades, and be replaced by grassland.

This would mean that the unbelievably massive stores of carbon currently locked away in the Amazon's trees and soils would rush back into the air, giving the climate crisis a huge shove in the wrong direction. And since the Amazon is probably the most species-rich ecosystem on dry land, the world's biodiversity would take a colossal hit.

The Amazon is the centre of the world ... If we lose the Amazon, that's the end of life.

OK, now I'm scared. What can we DO!?

Defenders of the World's Forests

Txai belongs to one of the many Indigenous groups around the world that are already leading the fightback. Though they make up just 5% of the world's population, Indigenous peoples care for 50% of the planet's remaining intact forests. Thanks to their ancestral knowledge, they usually understand how to harvest timber, food and other products in sustainable ways that let the forests regenerate themselves. And, crucially, their brave and tireless campaigning makes them the most brilliant defenders of these essential ecosystems. We should support them however we can.

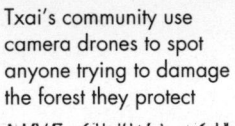

Txai's community use camera drones to spot anyone trying to damage the forest they protect

This battle is not just for us. It's for everyone.

Most of the world's governments finally 'get' the urgent need to protect the world's 'old-growth' forests. At the COP26 climate change conference in 2021, more than 100 countries pledged to 'halt and reverse deforestation' by 2030.

But as well as keeping the world's surviving wild woods wild, we need to grow a lot more trees.

Yeah! Let's just plant trees **everywhere**!

Well, that was the conclusion of a big scientific research project in 2019. According to the scientists' calculations, there's enough space on the globe for **a trillion** extra trees, and these new trees **might** be able to soak up **two-thirds** of all the CO_2 emissions from human activities that are currently overheating the planet.

I'm ready to start planting.

That's great! But, unfortunately, it's not as easy as it sounds. Before you start digging, let's hear from a scientist who can explain why.

THE HECTIC SOCIAL LIVES OF TREES

She's called Suzanne Simard. As a ten year old, back in the 1970s, she learned about every bird, beast and plant that grew in the ancient temperate rainforests around her home in south-west Canada.

All the plants and animals here are connected!

But when she got a job as a forester in the 1980s, she wasn't impressed with the way her bosses treated the trees. They fed them with artificial fertilizers and used *herbicides* to kill off any other plants that might compete with them for sunlight, nutrients and water. To Simard this seemed very wrong.

Remembering the woods of her childhood, where dozens of species grew vigorously alongside each other, Simard wondered whether different tree species really were always competing.

What if different trees can actually **help** each other?

In the 1990s, Simard designed a series of experiments to ask just this question. Her bosses were in for a massive surprise when she showed that birch trees – a species that they treated as a dangerous weed – might actually make the precious Douglas fir trees in their plantations grow faster!

Here's how:

1. Birch covered with a plastic bag containing CO_2 that is tagged with a harmless kind of radioactivity

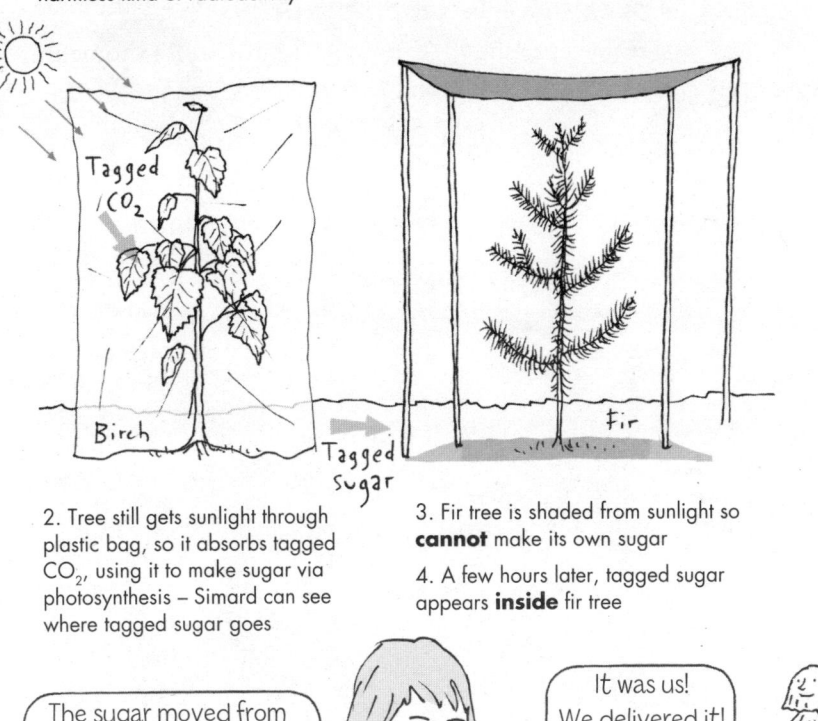

2. Tree still gets sunlight through plastic bag, so it absorbs tagged CO_2, using it to make sugar via photosynthesis – Simard can see where tagged sugar goes

3. Fir tree is shaded from sunlight so **cannot** make its own sugar

4. A few hours later, tagged sugar appears **inside** fir tree

The sugar moved from the birch trees into the fir trees, presumably giving them a boost. So how did it get there?

It was us! We delivered it!

That's exactly what Simard figured out next. Forest soils contain unimaginably huge numbers of fungal mycelia (see p. 8). They thread themselves round and inside tree roots, forming structures called *mycorrhizae* that are part plant and part fungus – most trees simply can't grow without them. What's more, mycorrhizae create invisible networks beneath the soil that move water and chemicals – like the sugar that travelled from birches to firs – between the trees that make up a forest.

> But why do the trees even want to share?

Here's what Simard thinks is going on with birches and firs in the forest.

In spring and summer

1. Birch shades fir (but fir still needs sugar)
2. Birch makes more sugar than it needs
3. Mycorrhizae carry extra sugar from birch to fir

> We make sure the trees share their sugars fairly.

In autumn and winter

1. Birch drops leaves (but still needs some sugar)
2. Fir keeps leaves year round so photosynthesizes through the winter
3. Mycorrhizae carry extra sugar from fir to birch

> And we get to keep plenty for ourselves!

Sadly, Simard's forester colleagues didn't listen. In the end she went to work as a university ecologist. But even there, biologists refused to believe her results at first.

Simard kept on experimenting, and slowly winning over other ecologists. Now, finally, most of them accept that she was right all along: every part of a forest is connected, like the different organs of a giant living body.

Every year now we learn more about the buzzing, criss-crossing connections and chemical 'chatter' constantly flowing between trees, fungi and other forest organisms. Some call it . . .

It's not a competition, Fungus, this is all about different species working together, for the mutual benefit of all. In fact, biologists call it *mutualism* – it's what keeps our world buzzing with life.*

*Find out more about mutualism in *Explodapedia: Evolution*.

Mutualism means trees need their mycorrhizae just as much as mycorrhizae need their trees. And, as we've just heard, healthy forests keep living ecosystems going across the entire planet. But it can take decades, centuries even, for a forest's 'wood wide web' to get wired up properly and realize its full life-giving, carbon-sucking potential, which is why . . .

We can't just bung a whole load of baby trees in the ground and hope for the best.

In fact, weirdly, planting trees can **sometimes** make the climate crisis **worse**.

Growing the Right Trees in the Right Places

You'd want to think twice before planting trees in a . . .

- **Peat bog:** Peatland soils contain more carbon per hectare than even the world's densest forests. Planting trees here can damage the peat, making it release far more CO_2 than the new trees will ever soak up.
- **Pale, sandy desert or icy polar region:** Dark surfaces soak up more solar energy than pale, reflective ones. That's why replacing shiny deserts or ice-covered ground with dark-coloured trees can sometimes increase temperatures and actually **cause** global heating.

- **Grassland or savannah**: These habitats often occur in dry areas, where wildfires are common. Growing trees there can suck water from the ground, making conditions even drier. If the trees catch fire, they'll send all their stored carbon back into the atmosphere.

But knowing about these potential pitfalls means we can focus on planting trees in ways that make a positive difference. And across the world, massive tree-planting schemes are underway.

In China, for example, since 1978, the Great Green Wall project has created huge new forests that protect valuable farmland, partly by slowing down the growth of the Gobi Desert. It hasn't all been plain sailing, though - lots of the trees died before they reached their full height. But in China and beyond, tree-planters are learning from past mistakes, and from the latest science.

Recent discoveries show that forests that spread and regenerate **themselves** almost always nurture more biodiversity and store more carbon than those that are planted. This kind of natural rewilding isn't always possible - for example, in places that have been treeless for very long periods, there won't be a supply of seeds in the soil, so some planting might be needed to get things going. But wherever it can happen, people should let it happen.

Too many of the world's forests are still being damaged and destroyed, but there are also huge areas, including parts of

India, the USA, Vietnam, UK and mainland Europe, where forests are spreading in the right way. The trees are on the march again!

CHAPTER 5
Why You Should Give a Dam About Beavers
A Wetter World is a Healthier World

In the far north of Canada, there's a dam that stretches for 850 metres. It's so big that it shows up in pictures taken by satellites in outer space.

What's the big deal? People build dams all the time.

People didn't make this dam; beavers did, using nothing but their chisel-sharp teeth, their nimble paws and their deep urge to construct. It must've taken dozens of beavers several years to create such a monumental structure.

> Impressive. But **why** do they bother to make dams?

Because beavers understand something too many humans forget: water is the most precious substance of all.

> Water?

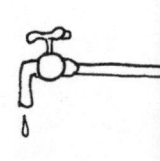

Yes, water. All living cells are full of the stuff – the chemical processes inside them would grind to a halt without it. Our friend Fungus can only force its mycelia through dense soil and dead wood because it pumps water into its cells at high pressure.

> GRRRRR!

And though you probably think of the human body as being pretty solid, it's actually two-thirds liquid water. Plus, water is utterly crucial for photosynthesis, the chemical reaction that keeps the entire living world going (see p. 37).

Without water, there can be no life.

> But there's water everywhere. Don't they call Earth the Blue Planet?

True, but almost all of our water is in the oceans.

> And have you ever tried drinking seawater?

Precisely. Seawater makes up 97.5% of Earth's water, but it's dangerous for most land- and freshwater-based life forms. There's so much salt in seawater that it actually sucks fresh water out of their bodies.

To see the tiny fraction of the world's water that's available to life on land, imagine it all fitted into a 50-metre swimming pool:

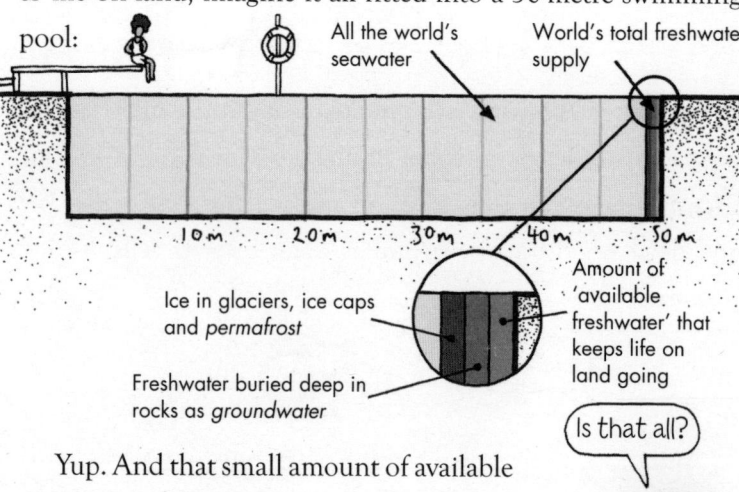

Yup. And that small amount of available freshwater has to be shared out between:

- Living bodies.
- Clouds (which eventually fall as rain).
- Rivers.
- Lakes.
- Soils.
- Freshwater *wetlands* (habitats that are either permanently or regularly flooded with water, such as marshes, swamps and peatlands).

Freshwater ecosystems only cover a tiny part of Earth's surface, but they contain a truly astonishing amount of biodiversity, including one-in-eight of every known species of plant, fungus, animal and microbe.

> So what's all this got to do with beavers?

A lot. For one thing, it reminds us how valuable freshwater is. The dams beavers build store loads of the stuff. But it's because of the astonishingly massive effects those dams can have on entire landscapes and food webs that we call beavers 'ecosystem engineers'. Their skills can really help humans too.

BIOLOGY'S BEST ENGINEERS

Let's take a look at a woodland stream before a family of beavers move in:

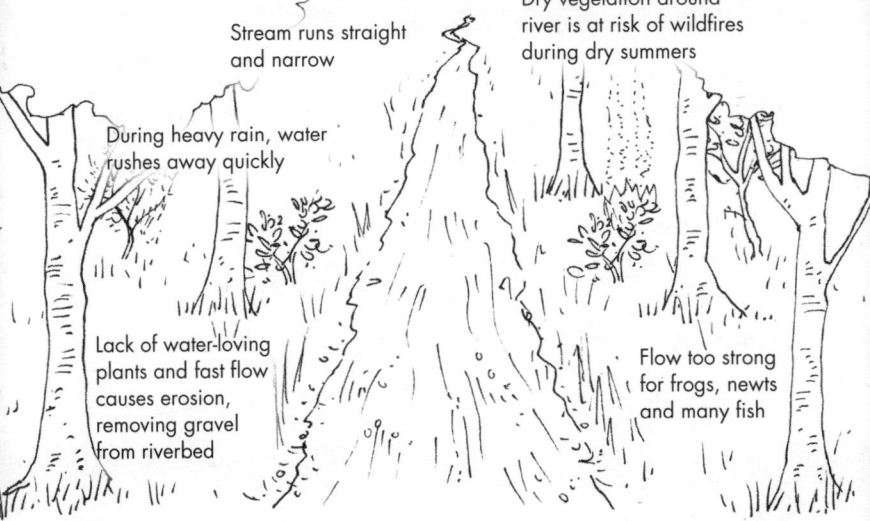

After the Beavers Arrive...

New marshy wetland provides food and shelter for insects, ducks, water voles and the beavers themselves (they're herbivores that eat tree leaves and waterside plants)

Beavers fell trees, creating sunny *glades* that encourage wildflowers and nectar-feeding insects

Water spreads into surrounding land, keeping forest lush and reducing wildfire risk

Shallow areas make 'gravel beds': perfect places for fish to lay eggs. Young fish feed herons and kingfishers

Dams create deep pools and slow, meandering channels

Geese lay eggs in safe spot – on top of beavers' dam!

Water bubbling over dams picks up more oxygen – it can support more life

Beavers' dam raises water level, so entrance to lodge is always under water, keeping beavers safe from predators

If trees die when their roots are drowned, dead wood provides food and shelter for fungi, beetles, millipedes, ants and woodpeckers

Most felled trees don't die – many send out new shoots and regrow

It's all so wonderfully wild!

It certainly is. These beaver ecosystem engineers have set off a whole series of trophic cascades (see pp. 45-6). They've invited dozens of new species into this habitat.

> All that extra biodiversity is lovely. But how do these dams help **us**?

Well, surprise, surprise, we humans haven't been treating the world's freshwater with the respect it deserves.

A Thirsty and Polluted World

Here's how we're damaging our freshwater ecosystems:

1. **We're using too much.** Most of the water we use comes from rivers, lakes, human-made reservoirs and underground *aquifers* (stores of groundwater inside rocks). In theory, these stores get replenished by the *water cycle*:

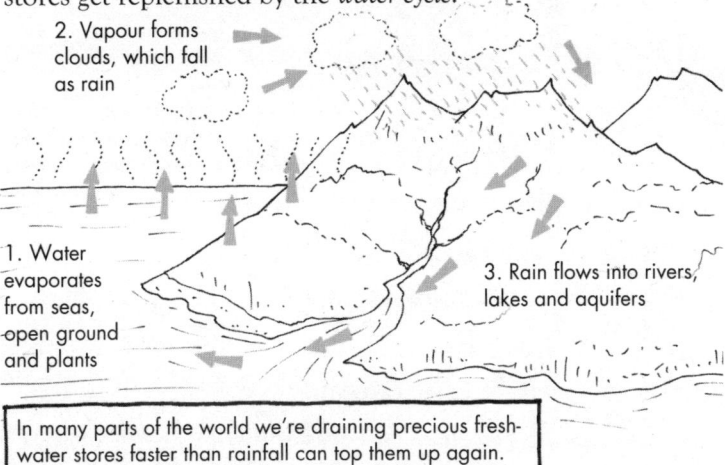

2. Vapour forms clouds, which fall as rain

1. Water evaporates from seas, open ground and plants

3. Rain flows into rivers, lakes and aquifers

In many parts of the world we're draining precious freshwater stores faster than rainfall can top them up again. Currently, over 70% of the freshwater we draw out of the world is used to keep crops and livestock watered

2. **We're poisoning waterways.** Fertilizers, pesticides, nutrient-rich soil and cow manure are all picked up by water flowing off farmland. Plus, all sorts of sewage and other pollutants enter the waste water that flows from towns and cities. When this contaminated water drains into rivers and lakes or seeps into groundwater, it can poison freshwater ecosystems and even create dead zones, through a process called *eutrophication*:

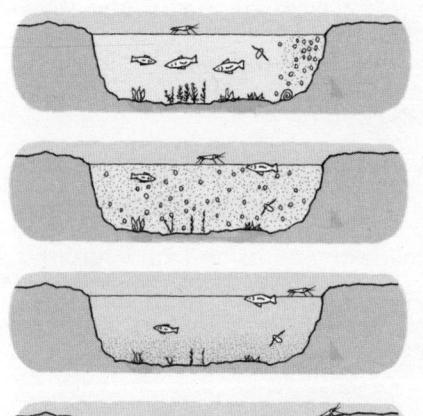

1. Pollution starts to seep into a healthy, uncontaminated pond

2. Algae feed on nutrients from fertilizer, sewage and eroded soil and begin to *bloom*. Some release toxins that kill other species

3. Algae die and the bacteria that break them down suck oxygen out of the water

4. Hardly anything can survive without oxygen. Fish and other sea creatures die or flee

3. **We're building dams.** Each year, humans dam hundreds of large rivers in order to store water in reservoirs and/or make *hydroelectric* power. Unlike beavers' dams, these schemes tend to destroy rather than increase biodiversity. When they aren't designed with great care, they can prevent vital water supplies reaching people, farmlands and wildlife – sometimes thousands of kilometres downstream.

4. We're destroying wetlands. Thirty per cent of the wetland habitats that existed in 1970 no longer exist today. They've been drained or destroyed to make way for fields, plantations, cities and factories.

This is all bad news for us humans. For at least part of each year, half the world's population can't get hold of all the water they need. But it's also devastating for wildlife. Populations of freshwater animals and plants are shrinking even faster than those on dry land. And there's no prize for guessing that, as the climate crisis continues raising temperatures and disturbing rainfall patterns, these issues are going to cause more problems and become harder to fix.

> So if there were a lot more beavers around... they could start reversing some of the harm we've caused.

Beaver dams even act as brilliant all-natural water filters. They can remove fertilizer, manure and some other kinds of pollution. That means less eutrophication and if the water that passes through beaver habitats enters our water supply systems, it needs much less treatment to make it safe.

> Why haven't the beavers been allowed to work their magic all along?

The Fall and Rise of the Beavers

Sadly, in the past, people have been beastly to beavers. By the start of the 20th century, hunters and trappers had very nearly wiped them out throughout Europe and Central Asia, and their populations were struggling in the USA and Canada. The hunters were greedy for:

• **Beaver fur**: Because it grows 100 times thicker than the hair on your head, beaver fur was used to make the finest, most waterproof hats money could buy.

• **Beaver 'castoreum'**: A yellow, oily substance that oozes out of glands inside a beaver's bum . . . Sounds gross, but beavers use it to mark out their territory. And – believe it or not – it was once used in human foodstuffs (including ice cream . . . yum!) and perfumes.

Thankfully, biologists have proved how brilliant beavers are for our world. And people are listening. Rewilders are releasing them into lots of their old habitats. In 1900 there were only around 1,000 wild beavers left in Europe and Asia. Today there are over a million, and counting. And they're all, err, beavering away, to usher water and life back into their surroundings.

Yay! We should reintroduce beavers **everywhere**!

Unfortunately, that just wouldn't work. Beavers evolved to live in the cool temperate forests of the northern hemisphere. Moving animals to new parts of the world they are not native to can be a risky business. The fragile ecosystems of Tierra del Fuego in South America suffered badly after 20 beavers were released there in 1946.

The beavers were being encouraged so hunters could trap them for their fur and castoreum. The beavers loved the climate and the South American trees – their population exploded. But the local trees hadn't evolved to live alongside beavers. The beavers' favourite northern hemisphere tree species regrow by sending up new shoots after beavers fell them (see pp. 81-3), but most trees in Tierra del Fuego **don't** do this. As a result, the beavers killed off large areas of native forest. The governments of Argentina and Chile are still trying to get rid of them!

So beavers alone can't solve the whole globe's water and wildlife woes. But we can put the things they teach us about looking after freshwater ecosystems into practice **everywhere**. We've just got to learn to . . .

THINK LIKE A BEAVER

The beavers' rewilding superpower is their ability to make water slow down and spend more time on the land.

Before it gets to your house, your tap water has already fallen as rain, which has run down hills and seeped through the ground. It's flowed into a river, lake, reservoir or underground aquifer and been through a water treatment system. Finally, it's been carried along water pipes to your home.

If beavers were in charge, they'd want to make that journey **even longer**, so that it passes through lots of wet and wild ecosystems.

Here's what we'd do:

Protect marshes
Like beaver dams, swampy wetlands are brilliant at straining pollutants – and even sewage – from the water

KEY
- sea
- marsh
- peat bog
- woods
- towns & villages
- road

Water that eventually reaches the sea will contain fewer nutrients. It won't cause dead zones (see p. 84)

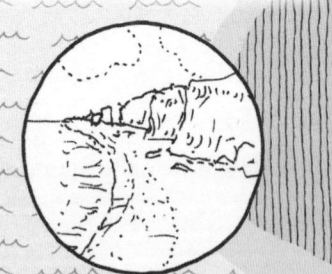

Build 'leaky dams' in streams
Water will move slowly, keeping neighbouring fields and forests *irrigated*, even in a drought. And when snow melts, or after a big storm, there will be less soil damage through erosion

Restore the river to its natural course, so it meanders slowly through valleys. It'll cause less flooding in towns and villages

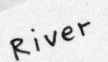
River

Protect peat bogs and woods
Hills will then soak up water like sponges and release it slowly and steadily

As the climate crisis bites and summers and dry seasons get hotter, we'll all understand why freshwater is the most valuable resource of all. And we can't expect rewilded ecosystems to do all the hard work of looking after it for us.

We need to demand that governments everywhere make and enforce strong laws to prevent all kinds of pollution, from pesticides to raw sewage, escaping into our waterways. And we can all do our bit by only using the water we really need – taking shorter showers and catching used water or rainwater to feed to garden plants, for example. It all leaves a bit more water out there in the world.

As the beavers have been trying to tell us for millions of years, a wetter world is almost always a healthier world.

Next stop, the wettest worlds of all: the oceans.

CHAPTER 6
Whales Are Climate Warriors
THE URGENT NEED TO REWILD THE SEAS

Have you ever stood by an ocean and marvelled at its crashing waves, unstoppable tides and far-off horizons? Earth's oceans are so massive, powerful and full of life that it can be hard to believe humans could ever truly harm them.

But we are harming them. And it's got to stop. As leading *oceanographer* Sylvia Earle puts it:

> *We need to respect the oceans and take care of them as if our lives depended on them. Because they do.*

It's a fact that more people have visited outer space than have ventured into the deepest parts of the seas. And because there's so much we **don't** know about the oceans, it's hard to understand how our actions are affecting them – and how we can put things right.

But, thanks to Earle and her scientific colleagues all over the world, our knowledge about the oceans is growing faster than ever. Each year we see more clearly why a healthy planet depends on healthy oceans.

Until very recently, for example, nobody knew about . . .

THE IINCREDIBLE LIFE-GIVING POWER OF PINK POO

Blue whales are the biggest animals that have **ever** lived. A large one weighs the same as thirty elephants, or three *Diplodocuses*. A whale catches krill by taking vast mouthfuls of sea water,

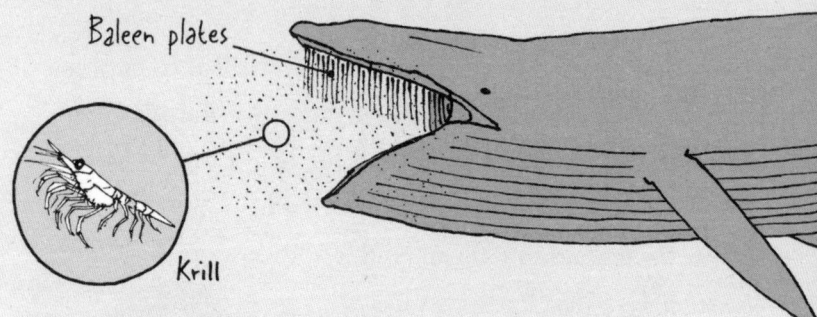

then straining it through bristly, comb-like 'baleen plates' that grow from its top jaw. It needs to eat a **lot** of krill, but exactly how much **was** a bit of a mystery.

Then, in 2021, using drone cameras, motion sensors (attached to whales with suction cups) and *echo sounders*, marine biologists finally proved that each blue whale can guzzle up to a whopping 16 tonnes of krill in a single day's feeding.*

*Because krill are a rusty red colour, they make whale poo pink!

It's hardly surprising that, as a result of all that guzzling, whales produce astonishing amounts of poo. And whale poo, believe it or not, is most definitely our friend. It can make a meaningful difference in the fight against the climate **and** the biodiversity crises. Here's how:

1. After eating, the whales head to the surface to breathe . . . And produce gigantic clouds of poo

2. Whale poo acts as a fertilizer, triggering massive blooms of phytoplankton (see p. 37)

3. Photosynthesizing phytoplankton suck CO_2 from the water and release oxygen

Phytoplankton

4. Blooms of phytoplankton inject huge amounts of energy and nutrients into ocean food webs, increasing the total amount of ocean life:

More phytoplankton → more krill → more fish, sharks, seals, penguins, seagulls, whales, etc.

5. At each trophic level, some creatures are eaten or die

6. Dead bodies, poo and other waste sink to the ocean floor, leading to the build-up of sediment

Scientists estimate that ocean floor sediments store **twice as much carbon as the world's soils** (see pp. 62-3). Most of the carbon in this sediment started out as CO_2 that was sucked out of the water by phytoplankton

By gobbling up so much krill – and pumping out almost as much *fertile* poo – feeding whales are constantly creating the right conditions for making more phytoplankton and therefore more krill. And that's not just good for whales, it's good for the oceans and for all of us – blooms of phytoplankton, for example, produce more oxygen than all the world's forests combined.

All these poo-related discoveries would be even more encouraging if there were still as many whales in our oceans today as there once were.

Sailors visiting the Southern Ocean in the 1700s returned home with tales of seas chock full of whales, feeding on swarms of krill so huge that they turned the water red.

But when the Industrial Age got going (see pp. 21-2), people discovered that whale fat, called blubber, could be turned into whale oil. And whale oil, it seemed, had hundreds of uses, from fuelling oil lamps to lubricating engines, factory machines and guns, to making all kinds of new household products, including margarine, soap and ice cream. The oil became so

valuable that hunters harpooned whales by the million. By the start of the 20th century, several species, including blue whales, were dangerously close to extinction.

Most countries didn't stop whaling until an agreement was struck in 1985. Today, many whale populations are slowly starting to grow again . . . But the trouble is, whales aren't the only wild sea creatures we've been hunting with reckless enthusiasm . . .

THE GREAT DE-WILDING OF THE SEAS

If anyone ever tries to cheer you up by saying 'Never mind, there are plenty more fish in the sea!' you can tell them that it isn't always true any more, partly because of a fishing method called 'bottom trawling'.

Sylvia Earle says this kind of fishing is like:

> Bulldozing our way through rainforests in order to catch the song birds!

It's a terrifying, but fair, comparison. Imagine if someone really did snatch millions of song birds from the wild and sold their meat to shops and restaurants ... We'd be outraged!

> But we think it's OK to gorge ourselves on wild fish!

How bottom trawling works:

Net scrapes along the sea bed, killing corals and other organisms

It snatches up all but the smallest creatures

Later, unwanted sea life is usually thrown overboard, often dead

As tall as a three-storey house

We have, in fact, caused the populations of many types of fish to plummet. Although today's fishing boats are bigger and more efficient than ever, they're actually catching far fewer fish, on average, than sailing boats with small nets did 120 years ago.

We've eaten our way through the seas!

What's more, in 2021 scientists estimated that the thousands of trawler ships that disturb the seabed are causing ocean sediments to release as much CO_2 as all the world's aeroplanes combined!

That's a horrifying statistic. We should be looking after our oceans, not stripping them of life. Because, when it comes to confronting the climate crisis, we desperately need their help.

Some of this stuff is seriously hard to take, but keep reading, there's good news to come.

As long as a football pitch

Disturbs ocean sediments, releasing huge amounts of CO_2

The Oceans Keep Our Planet Cool . . . So Far

Ever wondered why your kettle takes quite so long to boil? It's because water heats up far more slowly than air. This scientific fact explains how the oceans have managed to absorb an incredible 93% of the extra heat trapped by human-made greenhouse gases since 1955, yet 'only' heat up by less than one degree Celsius, on average. If all that heat had gone into the atmosphere instead, our climate would be a truly hellish **36 degrees** Celsius hotter than it is today.

But even a small amount of ocean heating has dangerous consequences:

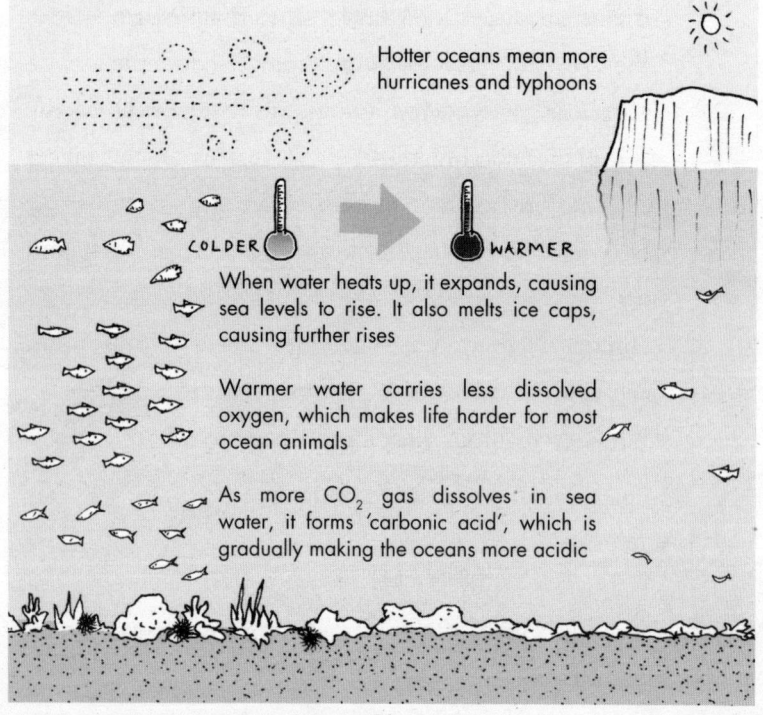

Hotter oceans mean more hurricanes and typhoons

When water heats up, it expands, causing sea levels to rise. It also melts ice caps, causing further rises

Warmer water carries less dissolved oxygen, which makes life harder for most ocean animals

As more CO_2 gas dissolves in sea water, it forms 'carbonic acid', which is gradually making the oceans more acidic

These changes are bad news for everyone, but they're particularly bad for coral reefs. Like rainforests, most coral reefs grow slowly, over centuries or millennia, locking down carbon and providing food and shelter for a huge range of fish and other sea creatures. Tragically, these dazzling but fragile ecosystems are *bleaching* to death across many of the world's tropical seas.

That's just appalling. Didn't you say you had some positive news?

Yes, but first we ought to talk more about the millions of tonnes of plastic waste that enters the seas each year! Turtles and sharks are getting snared by it and sea bird chicks are dying because their parents mistake it for food. The Great Pacific Garbage Patch is a floating island of plastic three times bigger than France! And every part of every ocean now contains tiny fragments of potentially toxic plastic called *microplastics* and *nanoplastics* . . .

Then there's all the raw sewage and other toxic waste that we've been pumping into the oceans for decades . . .

OK, OK, we've got the picture.

Right. Then let's take a deep breath and look for some answers instead.

Please!

Five Reasons to be Optimistic About Our Oceans

1. **Rewilding the oceans might be easier than rewilding ecosystems on land.** That's partly because living things can just drift or swim from place to place and, when the conditions are right, repopulate areas that have lost their original inhabitants. Marine life forms are also incredibly determined.

For example, in the 1940s and 1950s the American military exploded 23 different nuclear bombs on Bikini Atoll, a tiny string of Pacific islands surrounded by coral reefs. It was about the most destructive thing humans have ever done to an ecosystem. But ten years later, the corals started to regrow. Today the Bikini Atoll reefs are teeming with life again.

1950s

Today

2. **'Marine Protected Areas' (MPAs), are being set up around the world where fishing is illegal.** By safeguarding areas where fish can feed and breed – basically letting them rewild – populations of many species can recover surprisingly quickly. These no-catch zones can even increase fish numbers in nearby waters that aren't protected, benefiting ecosystems **and** fishing communities. The MPAs established so far are a great start, but we need many more of them, and tough punishments for anyone who tries to fish in them.

3. **You don't have to stop eating seafood entirely.** We can harvest some kinds of seafood in more sustainable ways, by copying Indigenous coastal communities. They have protected the breeds of fish they eat for thousands of years. For example, when trapping salmon as they migrate from the Pacific into the rivers of the USA and Canada, *First Nations* peoples often release the biggest 'mother fishes' immediately. This ensures there will be more salmon to catch in the years to come.

New ways of farming seafood (*aquaculture*) can also provide healthy food without hammering wild species. But aquaculture farms have to be set up with care, so they don't release pollution and diseases into surrounding waters.

Farmed mussels, clams and oysters can be some of the most environmentally friendly foods of all – they just need seawater to grow. They can even suck microplastics out of sea water. Then humans can catch the plastic-laced poo and dispose of it properly

4. Wilder ocean ecosystems can soak up much more CO_2.
Mangrove swamps, *salt marshes* and *seagrass meadows* are all plant-based habitats that grow along coastlines or in shallow seas. Scientists recently calculated that they can all absorb CO_2 much faster than tropical rainforests, often storing their carbon for longer. This amazing discovery is speeding up efforts to protect and expand these habitats. Even better: they also support masses of biodiversity and protect coastlines from storms.

Slightly further out to sea, the seaweeds that make up kelp forests (see p. 45) can grow by up to 40 cm in a single day – much faster than any land plant. Researchers are developing ways to turn kelp into *carbon-neutral* food, crop fertilizer, carbon-storing ocean sediments or even *biodegradable* plastic.

5. Scientists are trying solve the 'global whale-poo shortage' – by sprinkling tiny particles of iron into parts of the ocean. Iron is often the main nutrient found in whale faeces that boosts phytoplankton growth (see p. 37). If this whale poo substitute works, it'll mean more krill and, hopefully, more whales. And if the oceans could once again echo with the song of millions of whales, their magnificent bowel movements could take over ocean fertilizing duties: the oceans would be wilder and better at soaking up CO_2, and the scientists could stop their iron-sprinkling.

Come on, let's poo the world better!

It might not work, of course . . .

I thought we'd done with the doom and gloom in this chapter?

Sorry! Let's all aim to be more like Sylvia Earle. She knows more than almost anyone else about the problems facing our oceans. But she refuses to let it get her down.

All this knowledge is our superpower! Nobody knew any of it in the past.

But we know it now. And that means we've got the knowledge we need to get the oceans teeming with planet-healing life once again.

CHAPTER 7
Can We Raise Woolly Mammoths from the Dead?
THE RACE TO STOP THE ARCTIC MELTING

Until we came along and started hunting them with our spears, traps and fire, Earth truly was a world of giants – the species biologists call *megafauna*.* Most continents had their own distinctive megafauna. For example:

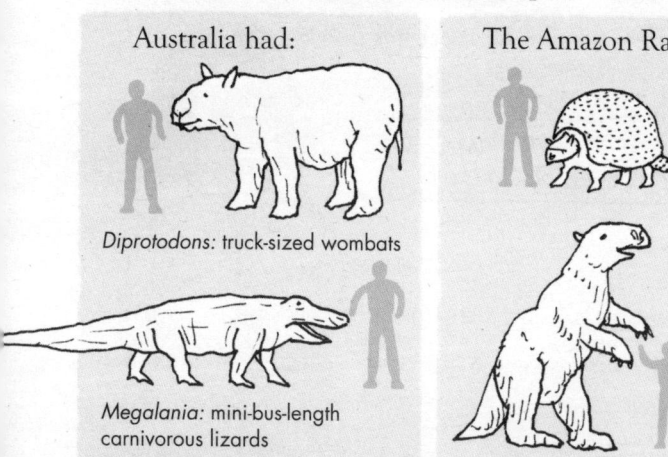

Australia had:

Diprotodons: truck-sized wombats

Megalania: mini-bus-length carnivorous lizards

The Amazon Rainforest had:

Glyptodons: armadillos the size of a small car

Megatherium: giant ground sloths as tall as a house

*Megafauna are often defined as animals the same size or bigger than a human.

Since the last Ice Age, one of the biggest impacts humans have had on the planet's ecosystems has been to help drive many of these majestic beasts over the cliff face of extinction. According to the *fossil record*, a region's megafauna often died out soon after human beings moved into the area. Just coincidence? Probably not. Still, overhunting isn't the only explanation for their decline – megafauna were also affected by past shifts in Earth's climate.

Because of their size, megafauna are often keystone species that have unusually large effects on the ecosystems they live in. By blundering around and guzzling lots of foliage, they can disturb dominant plant species, allowing other organisms to move in, increasing an area's biodiversity. And, just as whales shift nutrients around, injecting more life into the oceans (see pp. 92-4), megafauna on dry land can do similar things. Their 'mega poos' move nutrients **and** deliver plant seeds into new habitats, for example.

Sprouting seeds have their own pile of all-natural fertilizer

When the world's giants disappear, they leave giant holes in their ecosystems.

Which is why we need the giants back!

This is Eriona Hysolli. She's trying to do something most scientists say is impossible . . .

During the last Ice Age, large parts of Europe, North America, China and Central Asia thronged with mammoths. The last of them died out around 4,000 years ago, but Hysolli and her team are surprisingly confident they can give them a new lease of life.

The short answer is that some ecologists are convinced that mammoths can help slow down the climate crisis.

THE PERMAFROST 'TIME BOMB'

The longer answer involves the fact that global heating is causing average temperatures in arctic regions to rise around **four times** faster than they're rising across the rest of the planet.* That's why the ice caps are melting - and causing sea levels to rise - at an alarming speed. But it's not the only calamity caused by a warming Arctic: the region's permafrost is starting to melt too.

Permafrost is land that stays frozen all year round - apart

*This has several causes, including a positive feedback loop caused by melting sea ice (see p. 30).

from a thin layer at the surface that can thaw out, allowing plants to grow in summer. Arctic permafrost is massive: it covers a quarter of all the land in the northern hemisphere.

And it contains a truly colossal amount of carbon – more than twice the amount in the entire atmosphere. Permafrost carbon has built up over many thousands of years, in the form of soil (including peat), sediment and the frozen remains of plants, animals and microbes. So long as the permafrost stays really, really cold, the carbon inside it is safe. But as soon as it starts melting, decomposer microbes get busy breaking down the biological matter that's trapped inside it (a bit like when a freezer is accidentally unplugged and the food inside defrosts and begins to rot). The ground then starts to vent CO_2 and methane into the atmosphere.

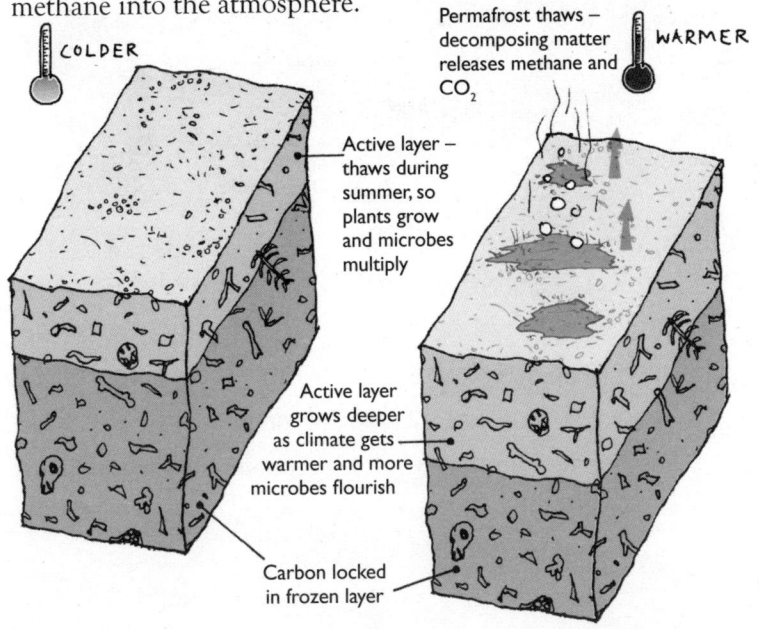

If too much permafrost starts thawing, it will drive one of those completely unhelpful positive climate feedback loops:

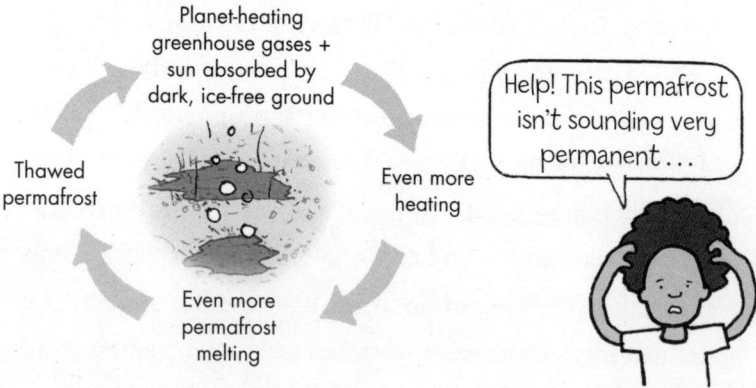

That's the exact problem. It's not! Because if too much of it melts, it could trigger an unstoppable thaw and greenhouse gases will start exploding out of the Arctic, making the climate crisis a whole lot worse.

THE GREAT MAMMOTH STEPPE

Back when huge herds of mammoths roamed the Arctic, their grazing helped create a cold, dry grassland habitat called 'mammoth steppe'. Snow fell on the steppe during winter, but in summer the surface of the permafrost thawed enough for lush grasses, flowers and shrubs to flourish.

Now the mammoths are gone and only small fragments of this once-sprawling habitat remain. Today, most of the Arctic permafrost is covered by habitats called tundra (no trees, lots of *lichens* and mosses) and *taiga* (forests of *conifer* trees).

> We're not trying to resurrect the mammoth for fun. We want them to regenerate the mammoth steppe.

And that, the scientists predict, would keep the deep layers of permafrost frozen all year round. Here's how they think it could work.

Arctic without Mammoths

In summer:

With few big herbivores around to eat them, more pine trees grow. Their dark needles and bark absorb heat, causing further warming

Less grazing → more trees and dry plants burn in wildfires → more warming and more carbon dioxide

Melting permafrost forms dark pools of water that absorb even more sunlight

Higher temperatures make microbes digest plant and animal matter really quickly, releasing lots of greenhouse gases

In winter:

Snow piles up and acts like a blanket, trapping summer's heat. Permafrost keeps melting

Arctic with Mammoths

In summer:

Mammoths damage mosses and knock down trees → grasses and herbs grow instead → pale-coloured grasses reflect more sunlight than tundra or taiga, reducing temperature

Intense grazing means less dry plant matter → fewer wildfires

Grass evapotranspiration (see p. 64) cools air, slowing down microbe decomposers

Mammoth dung fertilizes grassland → 100 times more plant growth (compared to tundra) → more carbon stored in roots, soil and peat

In winter:

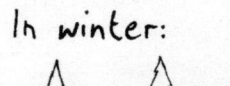

And loads more fungi!

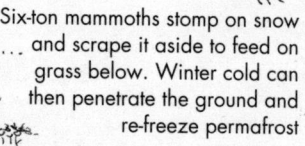

Six-ton mammoths stomp on snow and scrape it aside to feed on grass below. Winter cold can then penetrate the ground and re-freeze permafrost

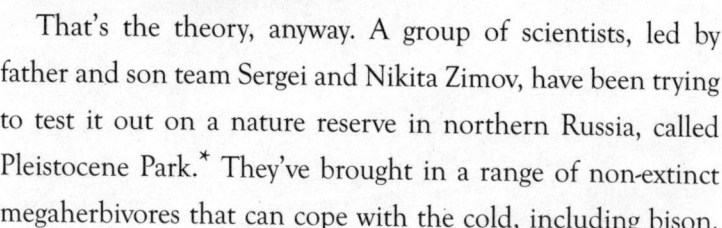

That's the theory, anyway. A group of scientists, led by father and son team Sergei and Nikita Zimov, have been trying to test it out on a nature reserve in northern Russia, called Pleistocene Park.* They've brought in a range of non-extinct megaherbivores that can cope with the cold, including bison,

---

*Named after the 1993 film *Jurassic Park*, but the park owners want to fill it with mammoths and other animals from the *Pleistocene epoch* (~2.5 million–12,000 years ago) instead of dinosaurs.

wild horses, musk oxen and Bactrian camels. Early results are looking promising – intense grazing and trampling by these big mammals really does seem to be keeping parts of Pleistocene Park's permafrost frozen.

How to Raise a Mammoth from the Dead

Here's how Hysolli plans to do it. She developed this method with her boss, a world-famous biologist called George Church, and it all depends on genes: instructions written in a chemical language called DNA. Genes tell all living things how to build and run their bodies.*

And since some dead mammoths' bodies have been preserved for thousands of years in the giant freezer that we call permafrost, Hysolli and Church now have quite a lot of mammoth DNA.

*Find out they work in *Explodapedia: The Gene*.

With the help of *DNA sequencing* machines and some fancy computer programs, the team have managed to 'read' most of the mammoths' *gene* instructions. And when they compared the mammoths' DNA to the DNA of their closest living relatives, the Asian elephants, it turned out they were at least 99.6% identical.

> So now we need to adjust an Asian elephant's genes so it grows up to be more like a woolly mammoth.

> Simple!

Hmm. Not quite. But thanks to a new technique called *gene editing*, 'adjusting genes' is much easier than it used to be.* Even so, it would be totally impossible to make **all** the elephant's genes match the mammoth's perfectly. Instead, Hysolli and Church are focusing on adjusting a few dozen, to give the Asian elephants the 'mammoth-like' characteristics they'd need to survive in the frozen Arctic, such as:

- Small ears – big ears lose heat too fast
- Thick, shaggy fur
- Blood genes adjusted for life in sub-zero temperatures
- More body fat for surviving long, harsh winters

> Bah! That's not a mammoth... It's a weird-looking hairy elephant.

*Check out *Explodapedia: The Gene* for all the details.

Yes, fair point. But 'de-extinction' is still impossible, that's why Hysolli and Church call their creations 'mammophants'.

And **if** their gene edits work, this is just the start. They then have to inject those adjusted genes into an Asian elephant *embryo*, and implant the mammophant embryo in the womb of a mother elephant hoping that, about 18 months later, the first healthy mammophant baby will be born.

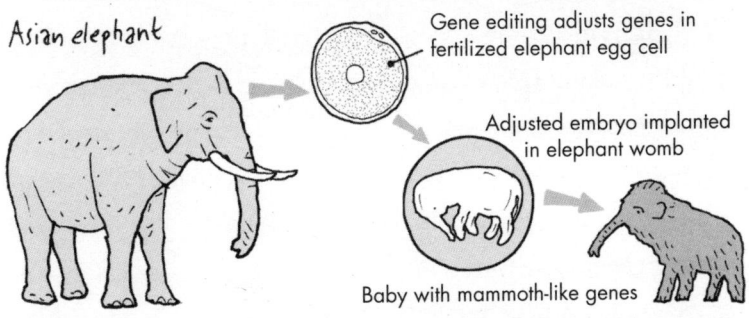

All in all, it's, ahem, a mammoth task. But Hysolli and Church are surprisingly confident they can pull it off. They reckon the first mammophant calf could be delivered by 2030!

Can We Rescue or Rebuild Other Extinct Species? Should We?

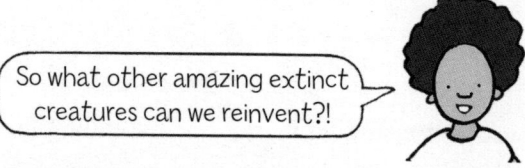

So what other amazing extinct creatures can we reinvent?!

Slow down a minute! Mammoths are a bit of an unusual case. Because they lived and died in such a cold climate, the DNA in their remains has been pretty well preserved. Scientists could try using DNA technology to bring back some recently extinct species, like *dodos*, because if their remains are stored in museums, they're likely to still contain undamaged DNA. But it's never going to work for truly ancient beasts, like dinosaurs – their genes have long since rotted away.

Aside from whether or not the mammophant experiment will 'work', some scientists say that adjusting dozens of genes all at once is too risky and too cruel to even contemplate. What if the gene-edited embryos harm their elephant mothers? What if mammophants are created but don't know how to survive in the Arctic?

There are easier and less controversial ways to use new scientific methods to help tackle the biodiversity crisis. Scientists can set up 'biodiversity banks' that store DNA – living cells, eggs, seeds and spores from today's endangered species. Then, if the worst happens and we lose these creatures, future scientists would have a possible way to reintroduce them.

Well, no, but hopefully telling people about the permafrost problem will help boost our efforts to radically reduce greenhouse gas emissions. And reintroducing big herds of slightly smaller megafauna species really could help regrow the mammoth steppe (see pp. 110-11).

It's impossible to foresee all the consequences of releasing large mammals into the wild. But sometimes doing nothing is the riskiest thing of all. Especially when 'doing nothing' means sitting back and watching great swathes of the Arctic melt and belch planet-cooking quantities of greenhouse gases into the atmosphere.

CHAPTER 8
How to Feed the World
. . . Without Wrecking Nature

We know we need to rewild huge swathes of the planet, but rewilding mustn't mean people have to go hungry. There are over eight billion humans on Earth today, and by 2050 there could be a whopping 10 billion of us. And everyone needs to eat.

> So we rewild **and** grow food. Simple!

Well, we've already turned over half of Earth's habitable land (i.e. the bits that aren't too frozen, sandy or rocky to support much life) into farmland - imagine one gigantic field covering North and South America and most of Asia.

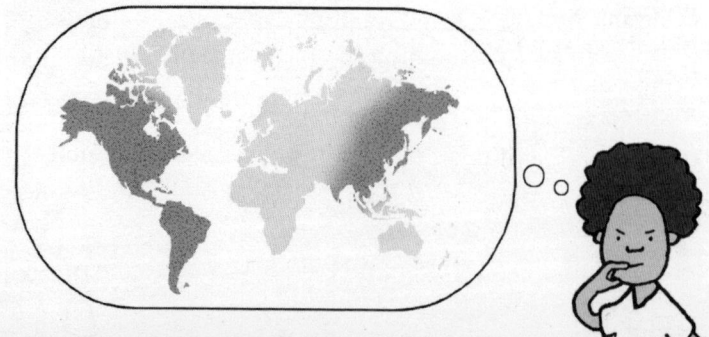

But hundreds of millions of people **still** aren't getting enough healthy, nutritious food.

Creating more fields to grow the extra food people urgently need is **not** the answer (see chapters 4 & 5). We really need to be giving quite a lot of our farmland back to nature.

> And the world's farmers need to do much more to help nature thrive!

Ah, Lady Eve Balfour, thank you for joining us. And you're right, today's farms are the number one cause of habitat destruction **and** massive sources of pollution, including more than a fifth of all human greenhouse gas emissions.

> But - as I've been saying for nearly 100 years - it doesn't have to be like this!

Indeed. Lady Balfour (1898-1990) was a pioneer of *organic farming* – a way of growing food that aims to keep pollution and harm to nature to a minimum. Most of our food is grown by *intensive farming* methods – which basically means doing whatever it takes to grow as much food as possible.

Balfour spent her life daring to think differently. First she shocked her *aristocratic* family by - gasp - wearing trousers! Then she shamed them by becoming a farmer. She started running her own farm during the 1920s, just as intensive farming was developing, and was appalled by the way many farmers were treating their land:

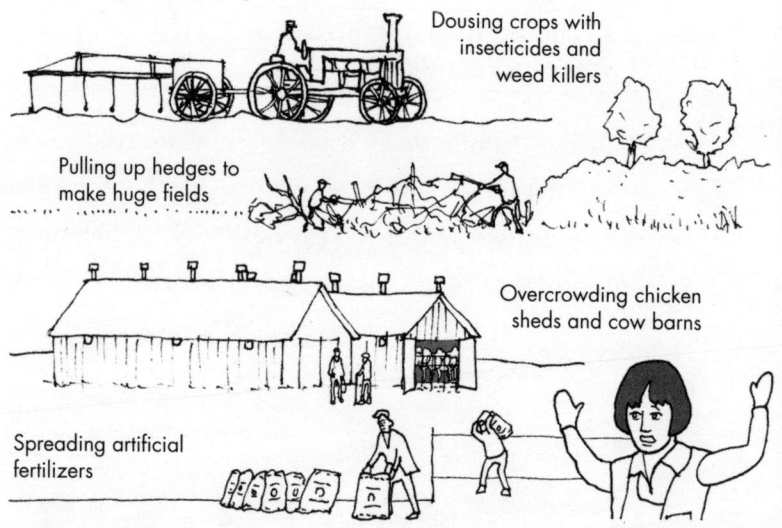

Dousing crops with insecticides and weed killers

Pulling up hedges to make huge fields

Overcrowding chicken sheds and cow barns

Spreading artificial fertilizers

Since then, intensive farming has spread all over the place, often becoming even **more** intensive. In some ways, it's been an astonishing success. Harvests from many crops have increased - there's no way the human population could have grown so large if they hadn't.

But environmental campaigners like Lady Balfour see it differently: the bumper harvests have come at a terrible cost - especially to wildlife.

Going Underground

Balfour proved it. She became an expert in soil science and used parts of her farm to compare organic and intensive farming. When she examined her organic soil, the sheer variety of living things growing inside it blew her mind. In her 1943 book, *The Living Soil*, Balfour argued that the **under**ground ecosystems these creatures form make soil *fertile* enough to keep most life **above** ground going.

Yup. Why not come see for yourself? If we head over to that organic vegetable patch we can hop into the shrinking machine.

It's just an earthworm... You've been through the shrinker, remember, you're 1.5 mm tall.

> Welcome to our world! Let us show you around...
>
> Erm... is it safe?
>
> That worm won't harm us. But stay out the way – it's busy.

Yep. Earthworms create tunnels that let air and water flow through the soil, preventing flooding and helping other creatures grow. And, after munching up biological waste, they help plants by pooing out fresh twirls of nutrient-packed soil. Earthworms are one of the soil ecosystem's keystone species.

But a healthy soil teems with far more animal species than any zoo or coral reef. Here are a just few of its amazing beasties:

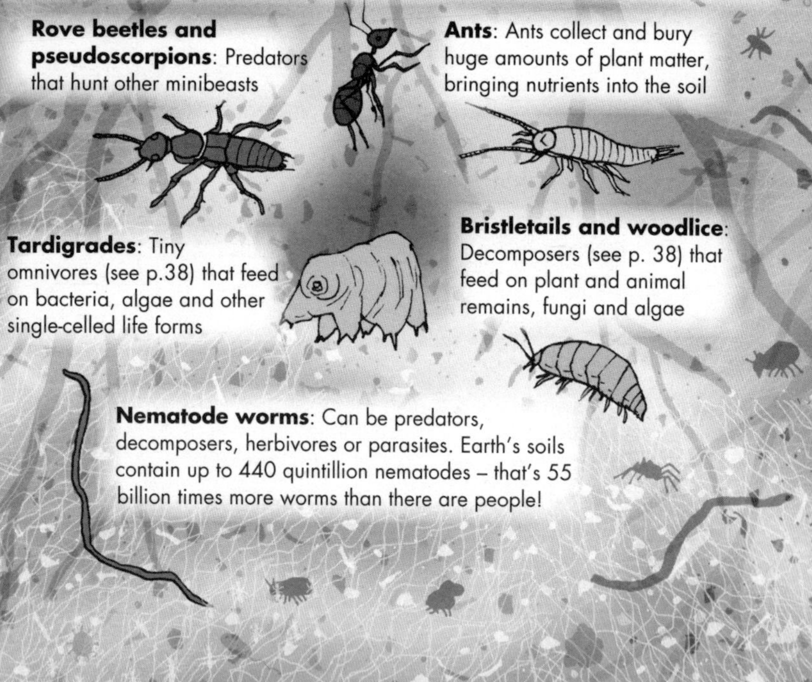

Rove beetles and pseudoscorpions: Predators that hunt other minibeasts

Ants: Ants collect and bury huge amounts of plant matter, bringing nutrients into the soil

Tardigrades: Tiny omnivores (see p.38) that feed on bacteria, algae and other single-celled life forms

Bristletails and woodlice: Decomposers (see p. 38) that feed on plant and animal remains, fungi and algae

Nematode worms: Can be predators, decomposers, herbivores or parasites. Earth's soils contain up to 440 quintillion nematodes – that's 55 billion times more worms than there are people!

Even the tunnel walls are interesting:

They're partly lifeless . . .

And partly very much alive.

Clumps (called *aggregates*) made of sand, crushed rock, silt, clay and bits of broken-down plant

Plant roots

Fungal mycelia*

So beautiful!

You finally noticed us! But we're not just here for our looks.

True. Fungi are keystone species too. They keep most plants going, through mutualism (see pp. 74-5). And mycelia bind soils together, stopping erosion. They also hold on to water – a healthy soil like this one will never dry out completely, helping plants survive even the driest weather.

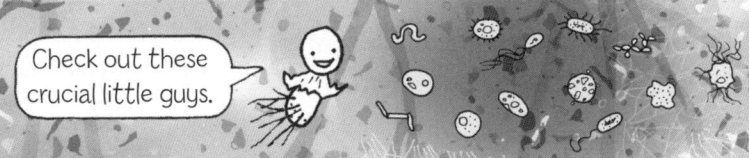

Check out these crucial little guys.

Yes, the bacteria. They're everywhere down here and they do a lot of the hard work – including making sticky 'cements' that build the soil aggregates. Some soil bacteria also protect plants from diseases.**

*If you joined all the mycelia in the world's soils together, they'd form a tiny thread that would stretch halfway across the Milky Way galaxy!

**Many antibiotic medicines used to treat bacterial infections originally come from soil bacteria.

And the 'nitrogen-fixing bacteria' are some of the most important life forms of all. No living thing can grow without a supply of nitrogen. It makes up 78% of the air in our world, but most life forms can't use nitrogen in gas form. Which is where the nitrogen-fixing bacteria come in: they snatch nitrogen from the air and turn it into substances that plants **can** use. If these bacteria suddenly disappeared, natural ecosystems would run out of nitrogen. Then everything would die.

> W-w-what? ...We really **do** need the soil.

Great! You've got the message, now let's flip that shrinking machine into reverse.

> That was wild!

Yup. Literally. Healthy soils are probably the world's most biodiverse ecosystems. The creatures inside them recycle waste, stabilize the climate and build the beautiful, bewildering complicated structures of the soil itself.

And almost all land-based life – including human life – depends upon that soil for survival. Over 95% of our food relies on plants that are rooted in soil. Which is the massive problem with intensive farming. It can end up...

Turning Living Soil into Lifeless Dirt

Scientists recently estimated that up to 30% of the Earth's soils are now so damaged by intensive farming that they struggle to support much plant or animal life. The damage can happen in various ways.

Ploughing too often or too harshly can:

- Kill soil organisms, reducing fertility.
- Make soils vent climate-heating CO_2 into the air.
- Break soil structures, making soil more likely to disappear – for ever – through erosion.

Although soil can heal itself, it happens extremely slowly; a layer one centimetre thick can take centuries to form.

And you lot can destroy it in seconds!

Artificial Fertilizers: In the early 1900s scientists managed to mimic what nitrogen-fixing bacteria had been doing for billions of years – turning nitrogen gas into plant 'food'. Artificial fertilizers can certainly make crops grow faster, but they also kill loads of soil organisms and can destroy freshwater ecosystems (see p. 84).

Ugh. We hate them!

And once the bacteria and fungi start to die off, farmers can only grow crops by piling on more artificial fertilizer.

Pesticides (including insecticides, herbicides and *fungicides*) are designed to destroy insect pests, weeds and plant diseases. But they can also kill all kinds of life forms that exist in and around the soil. Rising pesticide use is causing insect numbers to **plunge** in many parts of the world.

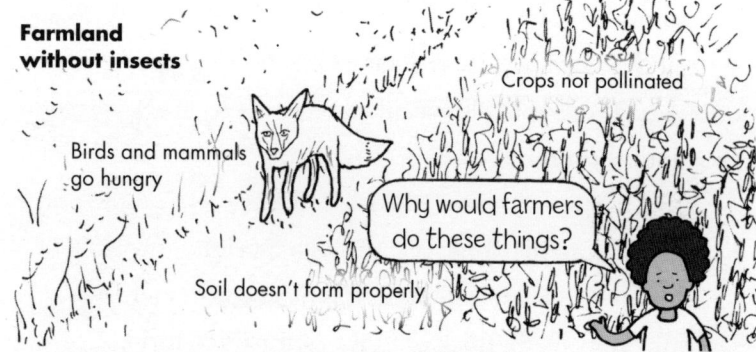

Well, they aren't deliberately **trying** to harm the natural world. Most farmers just want to grow the food that keeps us all alive as efficiently as possible.

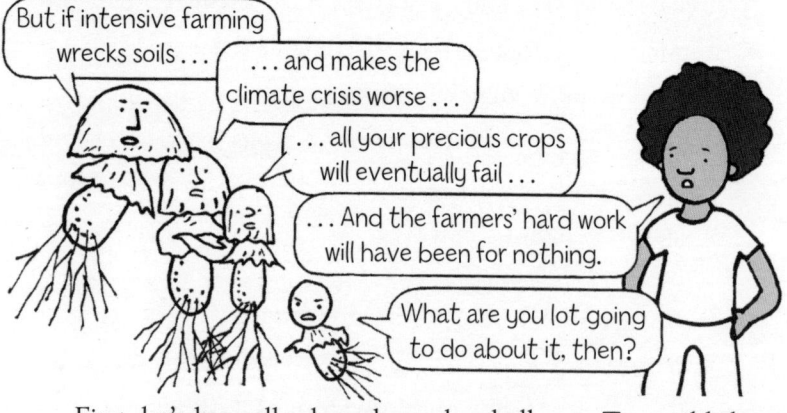

First, let's be really clear about the challenge. To rewild the

planet **and** feed the growing human population, we've got to:
- Grow enough healthy food for **everyone**.
- Use **less** land.
- Cause **less** harm to soils, the climate and biodiversity.

That might not be quite as impossible as it sounds.

Four Ways to Grow Food and Rewild the World

Thousands of people all over the world are frantically searching for solutions in these four areas.

1. **Land-sharing** basically means letting wildlife flourish alongside crops and livestock.

> That's what I always tried to do!

Exactly – organic and other *regenerative* farming methods are all about **rewilding the soil**. For example, by using composted plant waste and animal manure to build up soil food webs, farmers can increase biodiversity and improve fertility. Regenerative farmers also try to keep pests and diseases under control by mimicking natural ecosystems with:

A mix of crops and farm animals that make disease outbreaks less likely

Loads of insects to pollinate crops and build soil

New habitats for pest-chomping predators, e.g. wasps and spiders (see p. 58-9)

But regenerative farms often produce slightly less food per hectare than equivalent intensive farms. So feeding the whole world this way might mean we'd need even more fields, which could be even more damaging to natural habitats.

Land-sharing is probably only part of the answer.

2. **Land-sparing**, on the other hand, means using new technologies and scientific discoveries to make farming even more efficient, 'sparing' some farmland for rewilding.

For example, scientists are developing a whole range of new 'super-crops' that can:

- Make their own fertilizer, so they don't drain nutrients from the soil.
- Resist diseases and fight off insect pests without pesticides.
- Produce bumper harvests, year after year, so fields never need to be ploughed.*

The trouble is, most of these fancy new plants don't exist yet, so some environmental campaigners worry that asking farmers to make harvests even bigger could encourage them to pour more polluting chemicals onto their fields.

Noooo!

---

*Most food currently comes from annual plants that must be regrown from seed every year. Perennial plants produce crops every year.

3. **Waste less food**: Believe it or not, the world **already** grows enough food to feed the 10 billion people who could be alive in 2050. But, shockingly, around **one-third** of our food gets **wasted**.

- Some goes bad on the long journey from field to shop.
- Some is considered too 'wonky' to sell.
- A lot goes past its 'sell by' date and gets chucked.

If less food was wasted, farmers wouldn't need to grow so much, giving natural ecosystems more space. We can all do our bit by only buying the food we actually need and making sure every last leftover scrap gets used. Some companies are even:

- Turning food waste into plant-based building materials.
- Using waste to produce renewable 'biogas' for heating homes.
- Feeding waste to insects, in order to turn them into nutritious food for humans.

4. **Eat less meat and dairy** Another third of all the food crops we grow gets fed to farm animals. Some people see this as a kind of food waste.

But those animals provide us with meat, cheese, eggs and milk! How's that wasteful?

It's just not very efficient. Only a fraction of crops fed to animals get turned into edible food:

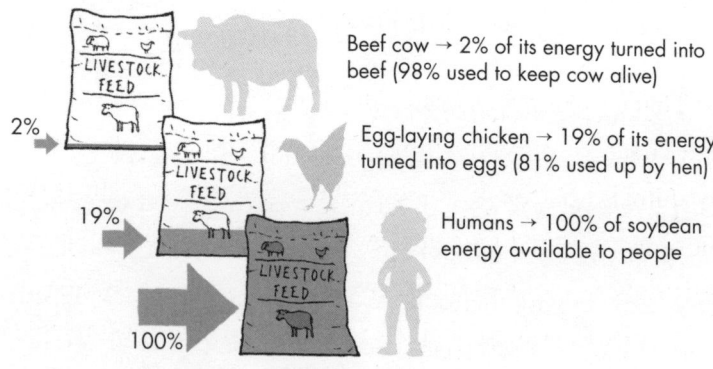

Sack of soybeans fed to:

- 2% → Beef cow → 2% of its energy turned into beef (98% used to keep cow alive)
- 19% → Egg-laying chicken → 19% of its energy turned into eggs (81% used up by hen)
- 100% → Humans → 100% of soybean energy available to people

Cows and sheep also use masses of land (that could otherwise be rewilded) and their burps are laced with methane, while all livestock dung and urine releases nitrous oxide gas into the air. And methane and nitrous oxide are, of course, two of the most powerful greenhouse gases.

Yep – it's hard not to believe that at least some livestock suffer. And, in any case, we certainly don't all **need** lots of animal-based food in our daily diets.

Well, growing beans and nuts is good for the soil* and they're great sources of healthy *protein*.

> But meat and cheese are so much more delicious!

That's a matter of taste. And tastes can change: scientists and chefs are busy dreaming up all sorts of new alternatives to animal-based food. Some of these new foods might take a bit of getting used to, but they could be just as delicious and nutritious as your familiar favourites today. For example, a company in Finland is actually trying to turn thin air into food. Here's how:

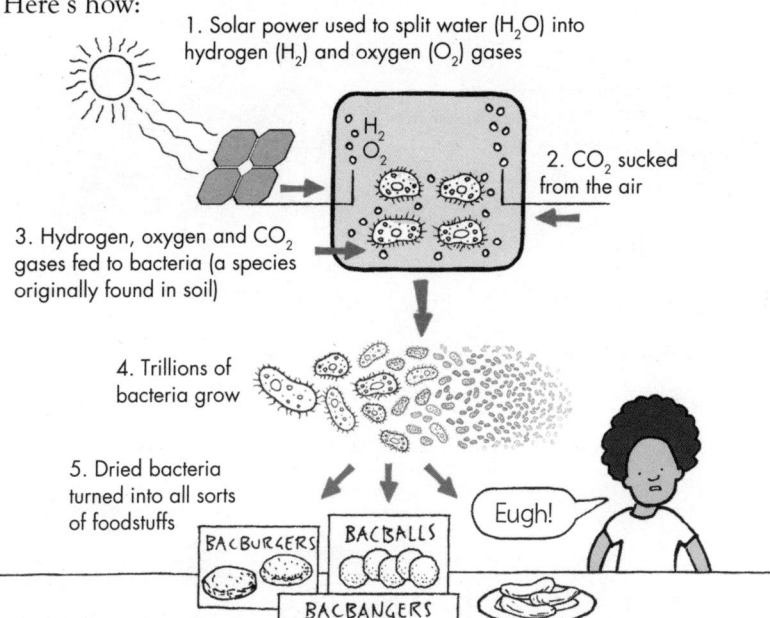

1. Solar power used to split water (H_2O) into hydrogen (H_2) and oxygen (O_2) gases
2. CO_2 sucked from the air
3. Hydrogen, oxygen and CO_2 gases fed to bacteria (a species originally found in soil)
4. Trillions of bacteria grow
5. Dried bacteria turned into all sorts of foodstuffs

Eugh!

BACBURGERS   BACBALLS
       BACBANGERS

---

*For example, the roots of bean plants improve soil fertility by supporting billions of nitrogen-fixing bacteria (see p. 122), while most nuts grow on trees, which means less ploughing and soil disturbance.

But is eating bacteria slurry **actually** any weirder than gnawing on animal muscles (aka meat) and slurping down their 'mammary secretions' (aka milk)? Either way, the fact is, if everyone stopped eating animal-based foods, we could reduce the total amount of world farmland by a whopping 75%. Deforestation in places like the Amazon would stop overnight (see pp. 66-8)!

And nature could go absolutely wild!

It's never as simple as it sounds though. Some farmers say animal farming is essential, and not just because they're hooked on cheese and bacon . . .

Well, animal manure does keep organic soils fertile. And . . . have you ever tried eating grass?

Nope. But grazing animals can indeed turn totally inedible plant matter into nutrient-rich food. In parts of the world where growing crops is tricky, livestock literally keep people alive. Plus, big grazing herbivores, like cows, horses and buffaloes, are helping some rewilding projects (see pp. 110-11).

Sigh. Why is nothing ever straightforward?

THERE ARE ANSWERS OUT THERE

Don't despair! There was never going to be one magical solution to all our food-growing and rewilding woes. And, as we've just heard, loads of people are busy hatching bright ideas that could help. Now they've got to work with scientists to make sure their solutions:

- ✔ Produce healthy food at a fair price for growers **and** shoppers.
- ✔ Reduce pollution and greenhouse gases.
- ✔ Stop habitat destruction.
- ✔ Let wild ecosystems grow.
- ✔ Protect the soil.

That last point is particularly crucial. Because . . .

> Without the living soil there can be no life on land!

Precisely. We can only rewild Earth by rewilding the earth.

> Yeeessss! Just give us the chance . . .

> . . . and the mighty mycelia will come!

CHAPTER 9
How You Can Help the Wild
... AND THE WILD CAN HELP YOU

So now we understand how rewilding works. And we know that wild creatures can do an incredible job of coaxing life back into our damaged world.

> But I'm still feeling stressed out by the state of things.

> Good! You should be! You've really mucked the place up.

> And you're running out of time to fix it.

Calm, Fungus. Yes, we've got loads to do. But making individual people feel **responsible** for the enormous challenges facing nature isn't helpful. The fact is, masses of people are already so concerned that they're suffering from 'eco-anxiety' –

a mental-health condition involving overwhelming feelings of anger, guilt and despair. More worry is the last thing we need.

Even our best-known and most brilliant climate campaigner to date, Greta Thunberg, has struggled with eco-anxiety since she was eight. Her teacher showed the class a documentary about climate change that made her so furious – and so depressed – that in the end . . .

> I hardly spoke for three years.

But Thunberg transformed her pain into **action**. In 2018 she started protesting outside the Swedish parliament every Friday, demanding her government do more to tackle the climate crisis. Greta called this a school strike for the climate (even though she kept up with her schoolwork). Gradually, more and more people joined her until, on 20th September 2019, Fridays for Future protests involving four million young people took place in 161 different countries.

Precisely. And these five steps might get you going . . .

Step 1. Spend More Time in the Wild

> How can hanging out in the woods be helpful?

If you really want to make a difference, learn as much as you can about the natural world by getting to know wild things and wild places up close.

> But I live in the middle of a city!

You and 58% of all humans! Most of us spend our time indoors, staring at our screens and travel along concrete streets when we do go outside.

If you can get to the woods or down to the coast to poke around in tide pools, do it. But what's also great is that loads of cities are discovering the benefits of 'urban rewilding'.

Dozens of Chinese cities are being turned into 'sponge cities', for example, that are designed to stop flooding and clean up water systems (see pp. 88-9).

Solar panels

Natural, water-absorbing street surfaces

Green walls

Plenty of wildlife

Vertical farms

Huge wetland habitats

None of that's going on in my city.

Don't worry. Wild creatures are constantly popping up around us (see pp. 7-9). Sometimes we've just got to slow down and make ourselves notice them.

Ants are so cool!... But is staring at this stuff really going to save the world?

Being out in the wild is good for you. Scientists in Japan, for example, recently proved that just being near trees helps your mental and physical health. That's partly down to chemicals called 'phytoncides' that trees release into the air around them. Phytoncides evolved to help the trees fight off insect pests and diseases. But when you breathe them in, they can:

Affect your brain, improving your mood and reducing anxiety

Boost your *immune system*, helping you fight off illnesses and infections

And if wild places help us feel better, we can fight a better fight!

Exactly.

Step 2. Grow Something Wild

If you're lucky enough to have access to a garden or a patch of school grounds there's loads you can do for wildlife.

Native wildflowers and shrubs give food and shelter to birds, insects, etc.*

Forget mowing the lawn and see what happens . . .

Pond made from old bowl

Decomposers and hedgehogs make their homes in piles of sticks and leaves

Online recipes show how to make seedbombs from compost, flour, water and native seeds

Throw them into empty corners and see how they grow.

If your patch ends up looking messy, well, good! Mess means biodiversity.

Mess means life!

If you don't have any land to rewild, try germinating native plant seeds at home. You just need a tub of soil and somewhere to put it.

OMG, I actually grew that!

*Ask neighbours if they have 'cuttings' or seeds to share. Search online to identify native varieties.

Even getting soil on your hands can be good for you. There's a kind of soil bacteria that can take up residence **inside** your body becoming part of your *microbiome*.* These bacteria release chemicals that, according to experiments on mice, can reduce stress and anxiety and improve problem-solving skills!

(Whoa ... I've never felt so close to nature.)

You **are** nature. Your body is quite literally a walking, talking, breathing, thinking ecosystem.

And if you ever get the chance to plant a tree, grab it!

(Yeah, but - really - a few extra trees won't solve all the world's problems.)

Imagine if everybody planted a tree. Or ten. Small actions add up.

Step 3. Find Like-Minded Friends or Join a Local Group

Thunberg started to feel better when she met other people who are just as passionate as she is. And Txai from Chapter 4 feels just the same:

(I get my strength from my people - and from the forest we call home.)

*Find out more about the microbiome in *Explodapedia: Evolution* and *Explodapedia: The Cell*.

Search online for environmental groups and conservation organizations in your area – protecting existing wilderness is just as important as rewilding new patches.

Teamwork makes great things happen.

Step 4. Get Political

Too young to vote? Your local politician's job is to represent **you**, whatever your age. So let them know what you care about by contacting them via letter, email or social media.

Scientists say the protests Thunberg inspired in 2018 and 2019 really did change the way people thought about the climate crisis. Millions came to realize just how serious our situation is. So peaceful protests are definitely one way to go – just find out about any potential risks before you jump right in.

But what should I actually be asking for?

Let's get some of the scientists and campaigners we've already met to share their rewilding priorities . . .

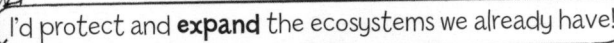

I'd protect and **expand** the ecosystems we already have!

Absolutely. Leaving rainforests, peatlands, wetlands, woodlands, grasslands, coral reefs, kelp forests, etc. **undisturbed** is the very best way to soak up carbon and prevent extinctions.

We should grow lots of new **forests!**

Yes! We could double the number of native trees (growing in the right places, see pp. 75-7) and plant huge seagrass meadows and mangrove forests along coastlines.

We've got to farm and fish in sustainable ways!

One hundred per cent. Over-fishing must be made a crime and we need to develop ways of growing food without shrinking or poisoning wild ecosystems.

And change the way we eat!

Not everyone needs to 'go vegan', but wasting less food and eating fewer animal products would mean some farmland could go back to the wild.

AND STOP FILLING THE ATMOSPHERE WITH GREENHOUSE GASES!

If we don't, all our efforts to protect and restore biodiversity could be undone.

Just. So. Much. To. Do.

There absolutely is. It's way more than any individual – even a politician or a landowner – can do on their own. It's more than any individual government can achieve. We basically need to get **everyone** on board to stop biodiversity losses. You might say rewilding needs to become second nature . . .

Which is why step 5 – which sounds so simple – might just be the most important step of all.

Step 5. Talk About Rewilding – a Lot

Let's be honest. As human beings, we're not the ones who can actually rewild the world . . .

Unlike earthworms, bacteria . . .

And fungi!

. . . we can't build up life-giving soils. Unlike trees and phytoplankton, we can't suck CO_2 out of the air . . .

Yeah, yeah, you need us wild things for all that.

But we humans **can** talk to each other. Conversations about rewilding won't always be easy – especially when we run into people (family members included) who simply don't agree that looking after the living planet is our top priority. These tips might help you handle tricky discussions:

• Listen carefully. Even if you disagree, never make anyone feel small or stupid – they'll dig their heels in further.

• Share some of the facts about extinctions and global heating you've read in this book, though the science on its own won't convince everyone.

• Try to focus on things you both care about . . .

That's just it! We need to talk about the sheer joy and sense of peace that spending time among wild things can give us. Stories of hope will help convince people to make more space for nature.

But where might those stories eventually lead?

Can We End the Anthropocene?

If we're truly serious about halting the biodiversity crisis and stopping the climate crisis from spiralling out of control, we need to stop thinking about ourselves as the only life forms that really matter. In short, we need to change.

> Ha! You lot - change?

We know it won't be easy, but we still have time. And here's one big, beautiful reason to be hopeful. When it comes to replacing fossil fuels and rewilding the planet, we don't need to focus only on the stuff we have to **give up** - the burgers we can't eat, the gadgets we can't buy, or the flights we shouldn't take. We can talk about everything we would **gain** from a wilder, less polluted world.

> What, like clean water...

> Breathable air...

> And a more stable climate?

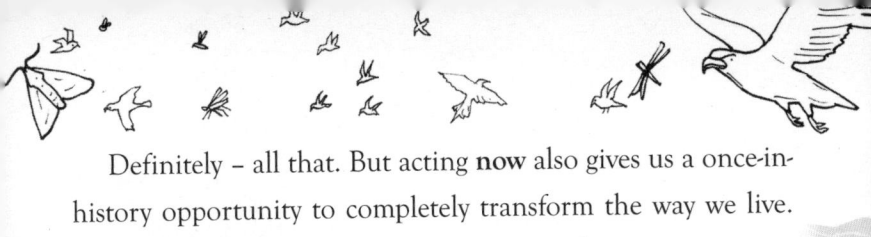

Definitely – all that. But acting **now** also gives us a once-in-history opportunity to completely transform the way we live. Now that humans understand ecosystems better, can nature inspire some answers to the biodiversity crisis – and make life better for everyone?

Well, we've survived... ...for hundreds of millions of years... ...without trashing the place!

Five Ecosystem-Inspired Solutions

1. **Endless Energy:** The sun pours far more energy into our world **each hour** than we humans use to power all our factories, cars, planes, ships, power stations, etc., in an entire **year**. And it's all totally free. That's why the plants and phytoplankton that keep food webs working will **never** run out of energy. The sun could, eventually, do the same for us.

Ha! We've been doing that for 400 million years!

2. **There's No Such Thing as Waste:** In the wild, absolutely everything gets scavenged, reused and recycled.

Thanks to decomposers like us.

So why shouldn't our materials for making new stuff come either from state-of-the-art recycling facilities, or new varieties of plant, fungus and bacteria that feed on what we've been calling 'waste'.*

New strains of bacteria break plastic down into its basic building blocks, making recycling easier

3. **Nothing Can Keep Growing For Ever**: Just as the otters stopped sea urchins growing out of control on pages **44-5**, we humans need to understand that we can't just keep on gobbling up the planet's resources. Technology can help by letting us do **more** with **less**:

4. **Diversity Will Save Us**: When bad things happen, biodiversity helps ecosystems keep going (see pp. 46-7). The same goes for diversity in human activities.

*Some of these could be made by 'synthetic biology'. See *Explodapedia: The Gene* for more details.

Imagine, for example, we all relied on nothing but wheat.*

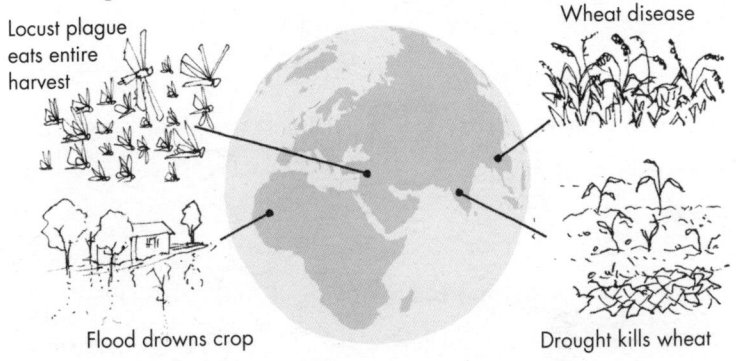

But if lots of different people grow lots of different crops:

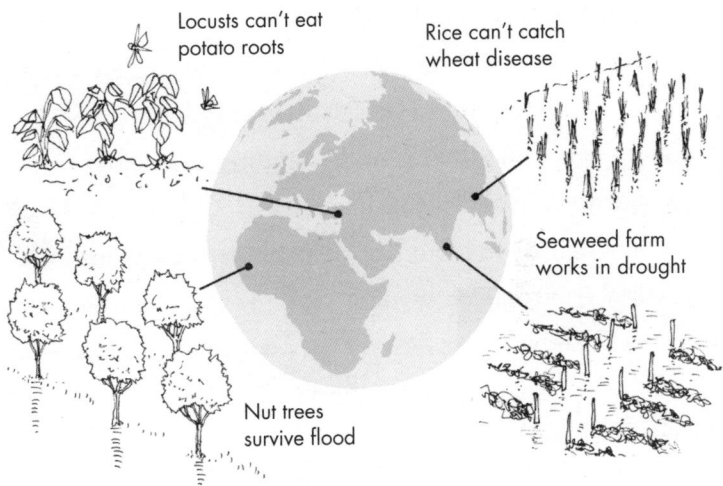

5. **Embrace Mutualism**: Just as trees and fungi help whole forests grow by sharing their resources (see pp. 70-5), we humans need to share ours. By protecting the species that help us and helping other humans too – especially those who've done less to cause the climate and biodiversity crises . . .

*In fact, the majority of our food comes from just four plants (wheat, rice, maize and potatoes).

Poorer places – some islands in the Pacific, for example – are generally being hit harder by rising sea levels and extreme weather. It's only fair that wealthy countries, which are more responsible for these problems, should help to find solutions.

We've still got a long way to go before we're even close to hitting E.O. Wilson's 'Half-Earth' goal (see pp. 14-5). But thanks to our ever-growing understanding of ecology, more people are finally realizing that it's 100% in our interests to look after our living, non-human neighbours. And, in 2022, 195 world governments made a vital pledge: to protect and restore ecosystems across 30% of the planet's surface by 2030.

Once we get going, making the necessary changes will get easier and easier. Eventually, it won't even feel like we're giving land 'back' to nature; we'll remember, once and for all, that we don't just **need** nature – we **are** nature.

Are you ready to see how incredible this place could be if we actually let the wild come roaring back?

Our Rewilding Planet – in the Year 2050

Welcome aboard our solar-powered, time-travelling airship. Prepare for some turbulence, as we zip forward into the future.

Before we arrive, a quick warning. Even if we achieve all our climate and biodiversity goals, the rewilded world of the 2050s won't be perfect. Average temperatures will rise, there'll be less ice and higher sea levels, and we'll never again see the thousands of extra species whose lives blinked out for ever during the early 2000s.

Hang on, we're here . . .

Earth looks AMAZING!

There's just so much wildlife!

The Arctic
A lot of ice has melted, but habitat protection and bans on shipping and oil drilling mean polar bears are doing fine

USA
Wildlife corridors let animals move between protected areas, boosting biodiversity

Atlantic Ocean
Whales are flourishing and helping to revive entire ocean ecosystems

Caribbean
Rewilding volunteers are busy replanting young corals

Huge new 'marine protected areas' (see p. 100)

Pacific
Coastal waters cleaned up by wetlands

Food grown on sustainable shellfish farms

Brazil
Damaged bits of the Amazon rainforest are growing back fast

Northern Europe
Plant- and bacteria-based diets and fewer intensive animal farms are sparing land for forest, meadow and wetland

Northern Russia
The mammoth steppe is growing fast, keeping permafrost frozen (see p. 108)

China
Urban rewilding means streets are now greener, cleaner and cooler

Southern Europe
Fruit and veg grown in organic gardens. Insect numbers soaring

India
Complete shift to renewable power. Robots help farmers grow more food and improve soils

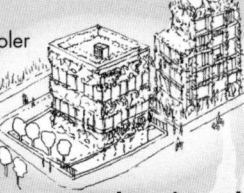

Indonesia and Southeast Asia
Preserving peatlands means Indonesia's rhinos have been saved from extinction

North Africa
Mass tree planting is slowing spread of Sahara Desert

East Africa
Reforested hills include areas for growing crops and provide cities with reliable water supplies

Australia
Reintroduced Komodo dragons eat invasive herbivores (see pp. 26-7)

> Can't we just stay in your future for ever?

'Fraid not. If we don't get back to the here and now, these changes might never happen.

DARE TO DREAM

Good things really are starting to happen, but we're still at the beginning of our rewilding journey. However, if we dare to dream, and are ready to put in the work needed to turn those dreams into reality, we really can steer things in the right direction. And we're not on this voyage alone . . .

> We're coming too!

Glossary

Words italicized in this glossary have their own entries below.

abundance the number of individuals of a species present in an environment

algae a varied group of *organisms* that *photosynthesize*, but are not plants

amphibian an *organism* that can live on land and in water, like a frog

Anthropocene epoch the period in Earth's history that started when human activity began seriously impacting *ecosystems* and the climate

aquaculture farming of fish, shellfish and aquatic plants, in water

aquifer a body of fresh water contained within underground rocks

atmosphere the layer of gases surrounding Earth

bacteria tiny, single-*celled organisms*. One of the main kinds of microbe

biodegradable can be broken down into smaller pieces by *bacteria*, *fungi* or other living things

biodiversity variety of life found on Earth

biodiversity crisis destruction and damage to natural *environments* that is causing species to go extinct and *biodiversity* to fall

bleaching when warm water stresses coral making it expel *algae* and turn white

bloom when pollution seeps into water, causing *algae* to grow rapidly

bryophyte the group name for non-flowering plants without roots – e.g. mosses

carbon dioxide a colourless *greenhouse gas*, formed from a combination of carbon and oxygen atoms

carbon-neutral when the total amount of *greenhouse gases* taken in and released is the same

carnivore an animal that eats other animals

cave lion a *species* of lion that went *extinct* around 14,000 years ago

cell the smallest thing that can definitely be called 'alive'. Cells live on their own as single cells, or together as parts of larger bodies

climate crisis dangerous changes in the global climate systems due to the warming of Earth's surface, caused mainly by human activities that lead to the build-up of *greenhouse gases* in the *atmosphere*

consumer a living creature that eats other *organisms*

conifer a typically evergreen tree that has cones and needle-like or scale-like leaves

dead zones areas of oceans and lakes that have low levels of oxygen, meaning few *organisms* can survive

decomposer an *organism* that breaks down and consumes dead animal, plant or *microbe* matter

deforestation the cutting down or clearing of forests

DNA sequencing the process of reading the DNA *molecules* that form a living thing's *genes*

dodo a large, flightless bird that went extinct in the 17th century

drought prolonged dry spell leading to water shortage

echo sounder a device that uses soundwaves to detect underwater objects or measure seabed depth

ecology the study of how living things interact with each other and their environments

ecosystem a community of *organisms* that interact with one another and with their physical surroundings

embryo a living thing going through its earliest stages of development

eutrophication when a body of water becomes too rich in nutrients, often allowing *algae* to *bloom*

evapotranspiration the process of water moving from the soil into the air, through land and plants

extinct when a *species* no longer has any living members

faeces poo or dung

fertile able to create or support new life

fertilizer a substance that makes soil or land more *fertile*

First Nations *Indigenous* people of Canada

food chain a sequence showing how different *organisms* get their food by eating each other

food web a system of connected *food chains*

fossil fuel coal, oil or natural gas made from the fossilized remains of plants, *algae* and animals

fossil record a collection of fossils documenting the history of life on Earth

fungal mycelium a network of tiny tubes, that forms a fungus's body

fungus/fungi e.g.- mushrooms, yeasts, moulds. *Organisms* that feed on decaying material or other living things

fungicide a chemical that destroys *fungi*

gene each gene contains a specific instruction for how to build a particular part of a *cell* or body

gene editing using technology to make precise changes to the *genes* of *cells* or living things

greenhouse gas a gas that traps heat in Earth's *atmosphere*

groundwater fresh water that seeps into the ground and fills up tiny spaces in rocks and soil

hectare 10,000 square metres

herbicide a chemical that destroys plants or stops them growing

herbivore an *organism* that feeds on plants

Homo sapiens modern humans

hunter-gatherers people who get food by foraging, fishing and hunting

hydroelectric electricity generated from flowing water

immune system network of *cells* that protects an *organism* from illness and infection

Indigenous people the original inhabitants of a place and their descendants

intensive farming growing animals and crops in ways that maximize food production, often by using a lot of machinery, *pesticides*, *herbicides* and *fertilizers*

invasive species plants, animals or other *organisms* that are not originally found in a particular environment and often cause damage

keystone species a *species* whose presence dramatically increases the *biodiversity* and resilience of an *ecosystem*

larvae young insects before they take on their final, adult, form - e.g. caterpillars and grubs

lichen a plant-like *organism* that usually forms a crusty or leaflike growth on trees, rocks and walls

mangrove swamp shallow, salty coastal waters where mangrove trees and shrubs grow

megafauna the large animal species that occupy a particular environment

methane a colourless, flammable *greenhouse gas*

microbe (microbial) a living thing that is too small to be seen without a microscope

microbiome a collection of different *microbes* that live in a particular place, such as the trillions of *microbial cells* that live on and in a human body

microplastic tiny pieces of plastic, smaller than 0.5mm in diameter

molecule two or more atoms joined together

mutualism a relationship between two different *organisms* that benefits both

mycorrhizae *fungi* that surround and exchange nutrients with a plant's roots

nanoplastic extremely small pieces of plastic remains, less than one billionth of a metre in diameter

natural processes interactions between animals, plants and the environment that aren't controlled by humans

nitrous oxide a colourless *greenhouse gas*

oceanographer a scientist who studies the ocean

omnivore animals that eat a variety of other animals, plants and *microbes*

organic farming a system that restricts the use of artificial chemicals, aims to maintain healthy soil and emphasizes animal welfare

organism a living thing

parasite an *organism* that lives in or on another organism and benefits from it, without giving anything back

pathogen an *organism* that causes disease

peatland wet, spongy land made up of peat (a kind of soil made from dead plants that have not fully rotted)

permafrost ground that stays partly or completely frozen all year round

pesticide a substance that controls or kills pests, such as weeds, insects or *bacteria*

photosynthesis the process through which plant and *algae cells* use energy from sunlight to convert water and *carbon dioxide* into energy-containing sugar *molecules*

phytoplankton *microbes* that live in water and harness the sun's energy via *photosynthesis*

Pleistocene epoch the period of Earth's history that lasted from 2.6

million years ago until 11,700 years ago

positive feedback loop a process through which a particular change leads to even more of the same change – e.g., a snowball rolling down a snow-covered slope keeps getting bigger and faster

protein a type of large *molecule* needed to keep all *cells* and *organisms* alive

regenerative to do with regrowth – e.g., regenerative farming aims to constantly make soil more *fertile*

rewild/rewilding giving *ecosystems* the help and space they need to grow more *biodiverse*, resilient and able to look after themselves, and us too

salt marsh spongy wetlands that form between the land and the ocean

seagrass meadow an underwater *ecosystem* formed by plants that grow in salt water

species a specific kind of *organism*. Members of a species have similar characteristics and shared relatives

taiga a forest of *conifer* trees found in cold areas across the far north of North America, Europe and Asia

tipping point the point at which a small change can trigger a sequence of bigger, often unstoppable, changes

trophic cascade when the arrival or departure of a species causes a series of bigger effects that spread through an entire *ecosystem*

trophic pyramid a diagram showing how energy moves through a food chain

tundra a cold, flat treeless landscape containing areas of permafrost, found in the far north of North America, Asia and Europe

United Nations an organization set up in 1945 to promote peace and co-operation among nations

vertebrate an animal that has a backbone

water cycle the constant movement of water between the oceans, atmosphere, freshwater habitat and land

water vapour when water has evaporated to become a gas

wetland land that is always wet or covered by water

wildlife corridor a link from one *environment* to another that allows wildlife to move without threat, safely and freely

INDEX

A
algae 13, 37, 40, 84, 120
Amazon 61, 64-5, 67-8, 104, 130, 148
animal products 126-30, 139
Anthropocene epoch 23-5, 142
apex predators 40, 56, 57
aquaculture 101, 148
Arctic 106-10, 114-15, 148
atmosphere 28, 107, 115

B
bacteria 121-2, 123, 129-30, 140, 144, 149
Balfour, Lady Eve 117-19
beans 66, 128, 129
bears 52, 54
beavers 51, 53, 54, 78-90
biodegradable plastic 102, 144
biodiversity 9, 10, 17, 32, 105, 125, 139, 144
  crisis 11, 15-16, 25-7, 46, 60, 93, 140, 142, 143, 145
  freshwater 81, 85
  ocean 102
  trees and 63
biodiversity banks 114-15
bottom trawling 96-7
bottom-up regulation 41, 42

C
carbon capture/storage 61, 62, 67, 69, 75, 76, 93, 99, 102, 107, 110, 139
carbon dioxide 28, 29, 61, 62, 67, 69, 93, 97, 98, 102, 107, 109, 123, 140
carnivores 38, 40, 56-7
Church, George 111-13
climate crisis 15-16, 25, 27, 28-32, 47, 55, 60, 61-2, 67-9, 75, 85, 93, 97, 106, 108, 124, 125, 133, 142, 145
consumers 38, 39, 40
coral reefs 30, 31, 99, 100, 139, 148

D
dairy consumption 127-9, 130
dams 78-9, 81, 82, 84, 85
dead zones 26, 84, 88
decomposers 38-9, 40, 54, 107, 109, 110, 120, 143
deforestation 25, 66, 69, 130
deserts 75, 76, 149
diseases 26, 42, 58, 74, 101, 121, 125, 126, 145
diversity 144-5
DNA 111-12, 114
droughts 15, 29, 89, 145

E
Earle, Sylvia 91-2, 96, 103
earthworms 119-20, 140
eco-anxiety 132-3
ecology 34, 146
ecosystems 12-13, 15, 25, 29, 32
  damaged 46-8, 56
  freshwater 81-5, 87, 90, 123
  keystone species 44-6, 105
  ocean 99, 100
  and predators 49-60
  soil 119-22
  solutions inspired by 143-6
  wild 131, 132-41
Elton, Charles 34-7, 39
eutrophication 84, 85
evapotranspiration 64, 65, 110
extinctions 10, 11, 15, 46, 56, 95, 105, 113, 114, 141, 147, 149
extreme weather 15, 29, 55, 146

F

farming 25, 66, 84, 85, 101, 117–19, 123–7, 130, 139, 145, 148
fertilizers 84, 85, 93, 118, 123
fishing 27, 96–7, 100, 101, 139
flooding 89, 134, 145
food chains 34–42
food supply 59, 66, 116–31
food waste 127, 139
food webs 36, 37, 46, 47, 93, 125, 143
forests 64–9, 76–7, 87, 139, 149
fossil fuels 29, 32, 62, 142
fresh water 80–90, 123
fungi 8, 54, 62, 63, 72, 73–4, 79, 121, 123, 144, 145

G

gardening 136
genes 111–13, 114
global heating 75, 106, 107, 108, 141
government action 69, 90, 133, 140, 146
grasslands 76, 108, 110, 139
grazing 108, 109, 110, 111, 130
Great Pacific Garbage Patch 99
greenhouse gases 28–9, 98, 107, 108, 109, 115, 117, 128, 131, 139

H

habitat destruction 25, 56, 66, 85, 117, 126, 131
Half-Earth Project 14–15, 146
herbicides 70, 73, 118, 124
herbivores 38, 39, 40, 41, 42, 109, 110–11, 120, 130, 149
human activity 11, 17–32, 69, 91, 105, 144–5
hunting 27, 44, 48, 50–1, 87, 95, 104, 105
Hysolli, Eriona 105–6, 111–13

I

Ice Age 18–20, 32, 105, 106
ice caps, melting 30, 31, 98, 106, 115, 148
Indigenous peoples 68
Industrial Age 21–2, 24, 29, 94
insecticides 118, 124
intensive farming 117–19, 122–4

M

mammoths, woolly 106, 108–13, 114
Marine Protected Areas (MPAs) 100, 148
meat consumption 127–9, 130
megafauna 104–15
methane 107, 128
microbes 10, 37, 54, 62, 107, 109, 110
microbiome 137
microplastics 99, 101
mutualism 74–5, 121, 145–6
mycelia 8, 79, 121
mycorrhizae 72, 73, 74

N

nature, rules of 33–48
nitrogen-fixing bacteria 122, 123, 129

O

oceans 13, 79–80, 91–103, 148
  effects of global heating 98–9
  rewilding 100
omnivores 38, 40, 120
organic farming 117, 119, 149
otters, sea 44–5, 46, 54, 144
oxygen 93, 94, 98

P

parasites 38, 40, 120
peatlands 15, 75, 80, 89, 107, 139, 149
permafrost 106–9, 110, 111, 115, 149
pesticides 26, 59, 84, 90, 118, 124
photosynthesis 37, 40, 62, 67, 71, 72, 79, 93
phytoplankton 37, 93, 94, 102, 140, 143
plants 40, 41–2, 105, 107, 121, 122,

123, 143, 144, 149
plastic waste 26, 99
ploughing 123
political action 138–9
pollution 26, 47, 63, 83, 84, 85, 90, 99, 101, 117, 126, 131
poo 39, 92–4, 101, 102–3, 105, 120
populations
  fish 97
  human 20, 21, 25, 116, 118, 125, 127
  large carnivores 57
positive feedback loops 30–1, 67, 106, 108
predators 49–60
producers 37, 40, 45

R

rainfall 65–6, 83, 85, 88
rainforests 31, 61, 64–8, 70, 139, 148
recycling 144
reforestation 69, 75–7, 149
regenerative farming 125–6
renewable energy 143, 149
rewilding
  how to help 134–41
  meaning of 13–14

S

sea levels, rising 30, 31, 98, 146
sea-grass meadows 102, 139
seafood 101, 148
sediments, ocean 93, 97, 102
sewage 84, 88, 90, 99
Simard, Suzanne 70–3
soil 39, 40, 54, 62, 63, 72, 89, 107, 119–25, 131, 140
solar energy 28, 30, 62, 75, 133, 134, 143
species 9, 10
  endangered 114
  food chains 36–42
  keystone 43–6, 47, 48, 105, 120, 121

steppe, mammoth 108, 109–10, 115, 149
sugar 62, 71, 72
Suruí, Txai 61, 68–9, 137
sustainability 139, 148
Svalbard 33–7

T

taiga 109, 110
temperatures, rising 28, 29, 31, 67, 75, 85, 90, 106, 107, 108, 147
Thunberg, Greta 133, 137
tipping points 31, 68
top-down regulation 42, 45
trees 61–77, 87, 109, 135, 137, 139, 140, 145, 149
trophic cascades 45–6, 54, 83
trophic pyramids 39–41, 42, 47, 54, 56, 60, 93
tundra 15, 109, 110

U

urban rewilding 134, 149
urchins, sea 45, 48, 144

W

waste 23, 26, 127, 139, 143–4
water 79–90, 121, 134
water cycle 83
water vapour 65, 83
wetlands 80, 82, 85, 88, 139, 148, 149
whales 92–5, 102–3
wildfires 15, 29–30, 31, 55, 67, 76, 81, 109, 110
Wilson, Edward O. 14–15, 146
wolves, grey 49–56, 59
wood wide web 74, 75

Y

Yellowstone National Park 49–56, 59

Z

Zimov, Sergei and Nikita 110–11

ACKNOWLEDGEMENTS

This book confronts some challenging realities. We've done our best to walk a helpful line between the horror and the hope. Immense gratitude to series editor Helen Greathead, designer Alison Gadsby and commissioning editor Anthony Hinton for your skill, dedication and creativity throughout. Sincere thanks also to copy and proof editors Julia Bruce and Philip Thomas, and to indexer Helen Peters. Working with the wider DFB team, including Fraser, Bron, Phil, Rosie, Meggie, Kate, Rachel, Kathy, Liz and David, continues to be a huge pleasure. Thank you also to ecologist and author Lee Schofield, for crucial fact-checking, insight-sharing and inspiration-offering.

BM: Boundless thanks to all the varied and wonderful wild things who entertained me, awed me and furnished me with life-sustaining 'ecosystem services' during the making of this book. Foremost among them are the rare and beautiful creatures known as Cal, Beda and Ghyll – I love you very much.

About the Author and Illustrator

Ben Martynoga is a biologist and writer. After a decade in the lab exploring the insides of brain cells, he swapped his white coat for a pen. Since then he has written about everything from the latest tech innovations to rewilding, running, stress, creativity, microbes and the history of science. He loves talking about science – and why it matters – with children and adults alike at science festivals, in classrooms or anywhere else. His writing appears in the *Guardian*, *New Statesman*, the *i*, the *Financial Times* and beyond. He lives, works, wanders and wonders (often all at once) in the Lake District.

Moose Allain is an artist, illustrator and prolific tweeter who lives and works in south-west England. He runs workshops and has published a book and an online guide encouraging children to draw, write and find inspiration when faced with a blank sheet of paper. Always on the lookout for interesting projects, his work has encompassed co-producing the video for the band Elbow's 'Lost Worker Bee' single and designing murals for a beauty salon in Mexico City – he's even been tempted to try his hand at stand-up comedy. His cartoons regularly feature in the UK's *Private Eye* magazine.